Is It Possible to Live This Way?

Volume 2: Hope

# Is It Possible to Live This Way?

## An Unusual Approach to Christian Experience

## Volume 2: Hope

LUIGI GIUSSANI

McGill-Queen's University Press
Montreal & Kingston | London | Ithaca

© McGill-Queen's University Press 2008
  ISBN 978-0-7735-3445-2 (cloth)
  ISBN 978-0-7735-3446-9 (paper)

Legal deposit third quarter 2008
Bibliothèque nationale du Québec

Printed in Canada on acid-free paper that is 100% ancient forest free
(100% post-consumer recycled), processed chlorine free
Reprinted 2009

McGill-Queen's University Press acknowledges the support of the
Canada Council for the Arts for our publishing program. We also
acknowledge the financial support of the Government of Canada
through the Book Publishing Industry Development Program
(BPIDP) for our publishing activities.

Library and Archives Canada Cataloguing in Publication
Giussani, Luigi
  Is it possible to live this way?: an unusual approach
  to Christian experience / Luigi Guissani.

  Translation of Si può vivere cosi?
  Includes bibliographical references.
  Contents: v. 1. Faith - v. 2. Hope.
  ISBN 978-0-7735-3445-2 (v. 2: bound). – ISBN 978-0-7735-3403-2
  (v. 1: bound). – ISBN 978-0-7735-3404-9 (v. 1: pbk.). –
  ISBN 978-0-7735-3446-9 (v. 2: pbk.)

  1. Faith. 2. Spiritual life – Catholic Church.
  3. Christian youth – Religious life. I. Title.
  BX2350.3.M36 2008          234'.23    C2008-900458-2

Typeset in Bembo with Futura 11/15
by Infoscan Collette, Quebec City

# Contents

# Note on the Translation

This work was translated piecemeal over a number of years, primarily by Dino Gerard D'Agata, Barbara Gagliotti, and Chris Vath. It was subsequently edited by John Zucchi. Lesley Andrassy copy-edited the final manuscript.

I have tried to keep the edition as free as possible of editorial notes, but it is useful to point out a few recurring names and an acronym. *Memores Domini* refers to a "private universal ecclesial association" (a juridical designation in Canon Law). Members are lay men and women who dedicate their lives to God. They are also traditionnally known as the *Gruppo Adulto* (Adult Group). Communion and Liberation (CL) is a lay movement in the Catholic Church. The author, Luigi Giussani, founded it in 1954, while he was a high school teacher. Originally he called it GS, which stands for *Gioventù Studentesca* (Student Youth). He often refers to CL in the text as "the Movement." For a brief overview of Giussani and his work, the reader might consult John Zucchi, "Luigi Giussani, the Church, and Youth in the 1950s: A Judgment Born of an Experience," in *Logos* 10:4, 131–50, or www.clonline.org.

John Zucchi
General Editor, English language edition

# By Way of Introduction

This is an unusual book. It is a kind of "novel," as those who first read the proofs noted. In this work the discovery of life as "vocation" comes about not through deduction but through the evidence of an experience lived according to reason, within the same breath as Mystery.

It deals with the path that Father Luigi Giussani took throughout a year in dialogue with about one hundred young people who had decided to commit their lives to Christ through total dedication to the Mystery and to His destiny in history. The Church calls this life "virginity."

Week after week the principal contents of the Christian faith and the reasons that sustained them were approached through a proposal that emerged from the author's experience and from the passionate dynamic of questions and answers that was awakened in these young people. Thus they gradually became aware of their human experience and lived it in a more determined way.

The style of these weekly meetings has been faithfully maintained in the book as a testimony to a particular approach to the great human problem and to the mature conviction and affection that it can lead to.

The book is not meant to be a challenge to common sense or to be presumptuous. It began as a faithful transcription of meetings and dialogues. It is thus a test or, better yet, a witness to a way of conceiving of Christian faith as something interesting, as a destiny for life. It is transcribed word for word, in its material immediacy. In that sense the repetition of ideas and formulae is aimed at filling one's memory in such a way that it might retain something that will be understood over the years and whose reasons will gradually be grasped.

The book can be conceived of as an exemplary narrative where spontaneity, loyalty, and seriousness in the consideration of one's own existence are able to ascribe a suggestiveness to something that most people would censure or disdain because of an abstract fear.

Is It Possible to Live This Way?

Volume 2: Hope

# 1 Hope

Let's tackle the second part of this year's meditation, which is a recovery of the fundamental words of our faith, that is, of the fundamental characteristics of our Christian personality. "Characteristics of my humanity" coincides with the "characteristics of my Christian personality." It's the same.

We've seen the first factor of our Christian being: faith, "the just man lives by faith,"[1] "justice is faith,"[2] true humanity is that which bursts forth from faith. We've struggled to begin to understand what faith is: if you don't understand it, you don't live. There's an understanding of faith that belongs only to theologians, to those who study, and that doesn't matter; no, it does matter! It matters, but it doesn't matter: what matters is what anyone can understand; and, in explaining faith, we have re-evoked what anyone can understand.

Hope is the other decisive factor for the construction of the Christian personality. If you have the Jerusalem Bible, at the back there's an analytical index and at the word "hope" it says: Hope – which is the fundamental word after faith: Romans 5, verse 2; and that could be enough. What does this little verse say? It says: "Justified therefore by faith [I'm not going to explain all the sentences now], we are in peace with God through the Lord Jesus Christ [these sentences are not understood, but they have a simplicity that arouses a certain reverential fear and a certain peace of heart]; through Him [this is the sentence] we have also obtained, through faith [that is, through faith in Him], the possibility of acceding to this grace in which we find ourselves, and of which we boast [what's the grace in which we find ourselves and of which we boast?] in the hope of the glory of Christ." It's a little terse – it's a thought that is expressed in few words, briefly – but it means that, through faith, we find ourselves and we boast – we are happy in front of whomever – in the hope of the glory of God. It makes this other flower or this other fruit come forth from the word faith; this flower, this fruit is called hope, hope in the glory of God. The glory of God means God recognized. Think of the last day in which everyone – those who are in China now, those who were in Russia during the time of Stalin – everyone will say: "Yes, that's right, it was just like this." They will recognize it: the glory of God.

"We boast in the hope of the glory of God": the aim of life, the aim of all the world's movement – as Leopardi puts it well in the hymn *Night Song of a Nomadic Shepherd in Asia*[3] – the stars that turn, the stars that are in movement … Everything is in movement – for what? And we know the answer, faith gives us the answer: for the glory of God, so that the glory of God is revealed. What does it mean for the glory of God to be revealed? If you don't know, you'll understand sooner or later: sooner means through a grace that God gives you down here, later means through an evidence that God will impose at the end. The aim of all the world's agitation, of things – of "this profound, infinite serenity," of "this immense solitude," the aim of everything, which moves itself slowly, more or less slowly, is the glory of God. This means all the world will shout: "The Lord is God, the master is God, the ruler is God."

Now we, through faith, by faith, live and rejoice in the hope of the glory of God. Through faith we arrive at an understanding that all this movement – the movement of the world (like the movement of my life, which seems small; *seems* small because for the sun to move, for the stars to move, for the galaxies to move, and for time to move, it's recorded by this small thing, my intelligence, which seems small, and yet it is large, because man is made in the image of God, he is the copy of the infinite), the aim of all this movement for which you get up in the morning (and that's a small thing – think of your little bed, that little bed from which you pop out like a little mouse; think of the sun that rises, of a huge bed!), everything that moves, faith makes us understand that it's for the glory of God, in the hope of the glory of God. Faith makes us hope to see that everything that moves, moves for the glory of God; faith makes us hope to *see* this.

The first way to see it, is to not see it; the first way to see it is to understand it, is to understand. Within sixty years, an earthquake will occur and half of California – excuse me, let's hope not, but it is possible, because there's nothing underneath California – half of California will fall into the sea. To understand this is much more than seeing it, so much so that by understanding it one can begin to put pylons in the sea, that is, begin to prepare oneself. To understand is more than to see. Who has objections? I say that without aggression!

In short, in Christian discourse, which begins with the word faith, a fruit immediately comes forth; there is, as a consequence, this new flower that is called hope, whose content is the glory of God: hope that the whole world recognizes God, hope that God makes Himself known to everyone and says: "I am," that is, "I have won."

Better than Romans 5:2 you can read the second letter to the Corinthians 3:12. Even here: "Strong in such hope [the hope that is born of faith], we're full of certainty." And here we had a beautiful moment demonstrating this, when we read *The Two Orphans* by Pascoli.[4] Pascoli's two orphans – who represent the world, how man normally lives – are full of fear, of uncertainty and fear. And it's easy for us to understand that if you go to them and give them a slap, a punch – whoa, now you're in for it! Those two timid ones, those two fearful ones, who speak like that in the poem, will cover you with punches and kicks, and their friends will avenge them; nevertheless, they're still two poor ones.

"Strong in such hope, we're full of certainty," we're not fragile like them, fearful, we're full of certainty. (Think, my friends, if he who wrote these words and I who repeat these words in his name, if we weren't aware that they adapt themselves well to you, because you could be highly insecure: not *full,* but *void* of hope!). I'm simply saying that the Christian is made that way: of faith from which the flower that is called hope is born and takes root.

Or read the first letter to the Thessalonians 1:3: "Hope [it says at the end of the discussion] that is the Lord Jesus." What does "hope that is the Lord Jesus" mean? Hope that is born from faith in Jesus.

Or the first letter to Timothy; precisely the first line says: "Paul [he speaks of himself!] apostle of Jesus Christ by the command of God the Saviour and by the command of Jesus Christ, our hope:" the word hope is always connected with Jesus.

Or 1 Timothy 4:10: "We labour and suffer reproach because we have placed our hope in the living God." The living God is Christ: another connection between hope and faith in Christ. I've cited these phrases deliberately to highlight the stated assumption: hope is, in Christian language, the second descriptive factor of a new personality; the second factor because it derives from the first, and the first is faith: without faith there is no hope; with faith there can be hope.

And since faith is the recognition of the great presence of God made man, we must try to understand now, to begin to understand the meaning of this word, hope, as the Church of God in the world uses it, as the great company of Christ in the world uses it, as the first apostles used it and as the missionaries who go to all parts of the world use it and as one who lives faith in Christ in his office or in his establishment uses it.

Now, first of all a definition. If faith is to recognize a Presence that is certain, if faith is to recognize a Presence with certainty, hope is to recognize a certainty for the future that is born of this Presence.

Faith is to recognize a Presence that is certain, like the faith of Monsignor Manfredini who, when he entered Bologna, a new archbishop, began his speech with these words: "Christ here and now. We should serve Christ, here and now; Christ present here and now."[5] If faith is to recognize a Presence that is certain, hope is to recognize with certainty a future that is born of this faith; faith is to recognize a Presence with certainty; from this certainty, certainty for the future is born. To recognize the content of a Presence that began two thousand years ago, to recognize it present now. What is this called? Memory. Therefore hope has a radical link with the word memory, so that without memory there can be no hope.

We hope to arrive at the eighty-fourth floor so that we reach above existing buildings before we hope to arrive at the hundred-and-tenth floor of the Twin Towers in New York. The hope to arrive at the eighty-fourth floor is based on the certainty of the eighty-three preceding floors. You can hope to arrive at the hundred-and-fiftieth floor if you're certain of passing a hundred-and-forty-nine first. Hope is born from the content of faith that is kept in memory, thus hope is born of memory, that is, of the consciousness of a Presence that begins in the past, of an "already done" in the past; therefore hope is that in which the past is finally fulfilled.

Certainty for the future is based on a present thing that you recognize with certainty; the certainty of a present makes you certain of a future. To be certain of the future, you have to be, therefore, certain of a precedent to the future, of something that precedes the future. Hope as certainty in a future thing rests on the entire Christian past, rests on the entire Christian memory, rests on all the certainty of that Presence that began two thousand years ago and has come to you. Certainty of the presence of Christ is certainty of a thing that began two thousand years ago; thus you can't have the memory of Christ as a Presence without in some way becoming interested in, marvelling at, being full of wonder towards, boasting about, being proud of, being happy about everything that happened in these two thousand years. The Church you have in front of you now, in which you believe, is the Church that has inherited two thousand years of history.

I understand your difficulty: certainty regarding the future, for example, certainty that the end of the world will come, doesn't rest on the present the way one stone rests on another stone in the building of a church or a palace – from an excavation comes a stone, you haul it on a horse or a truck, you put it on top of another stone and in this way the building is lifted to three, four metres. However, it is born in another way that we don't see, can't see. The certainty of my faith is born from yesterday, from the day before yesterday, from Saint Gregory the Great fifteen hundred years ago; it is born from Saint Iranaeus eighteen hundred years ago; from Saint Polycarp nineteen hundred years ago; from Saint John; from Saint Andrew; from Simon Peter. How is this born and how does it reach us now? We can't see it; we can know it though! Because with God nothing is impossible.

God is the master of time and space, while for us time is a prison. Time also offers a possibility of opportunity. If you didn't have tomorrow, you wouldn't be able to know another baby; if two years ago you hadn't had a tomorrow, I wouldn't have been able to know you, to know that there is a tomorrow; and how tomorrow is born from today, God knows, I don't know.

In these clear yet abstract sentences – clear though – is there something you don't understand?

*Does hope have to do only with the end of the world, the ultimate future, or does it also have to do with things that come before this in our lives?*
It has to do with the future. For example, the day after tomorrow what will you do? You will kill a man or you will perform a gesture of charity towards a man. I don't know, God knows, not even you know it now; this day after tomorrow weighs heavily on your whole future. The end of the world is simply the total flowering of the future, but from the initial bud to the wide-open flower all of spring goes by. We're speaking of the future, the words we use, we use in the same way that the dictionary uses them.

*I didn't understand when you said faith is born in a way
we can't see, but we can know.*

I have faith, I believe. You know I believe, you know that
a man can believe: yes or yes? But you can't know how
faith occurs in me, I can't even know it. And you, who
also have faith (I hope!), can't know, not even you, how
you manage to have it. Actually, it would be one of the
most beautiful revelations in your life, if you would be
reflective: why should this happen to me and not to many
others? And you are moved by the fact that God chose you,
He preferred you above so many others. And it isn't at
random; actually, from a very banal point of view, from a
"cartpusher's" point of view, it outwits you. God outwits
you because, if He gives you faith, He gives it to you so
that you carry it out, communicate it to others; that is, He
makes you an instrument of His mission.

What do you call that thing in man through which he
knows reality? Reason, which is consciousness of reality
according to the totality of its factors. If reason is consciousness of reality according to the totality of its factors,
if you recognize that I have faith, even if you don't understand how faith happens – you really don't understand –
you're forced to admit that there's a phenomenon that's
called faith. Otherwise, either you're a scatterbrain and
the word of your reason is a word at random, or there's
something you don't understand, but it's there. The entire
*Religious Sense* bases its demonstration of the ultimate
structure on this observation: you don't understand, you
don't understand, you don't understand ... by dint of not

understanding, you become aware, though; you realize; that is, you understand that there's something.

In what we've said, the most important words are: first, the word faith, to recognize a Presence with certainty; second, the word certainty, which has to do with the future; and, third, the link between the first and the second point.

Do you remember when Péguy said, in *The Portico of the Mystery of the Second Virtue*: "To hope ... one must have obtained, received great grace?"[6] What is this great grace? Faith in Jesus Christ; the great grace is the certainty of faith, that is like a tamarisk seed, one of the most beautiful plants there is. The tamarisk seed is small, a small seed that gets confused with the earth; with time it develops, it develops and out comes a large plant with that beautiful long hair, all rimmed with pearls that are little flowers, that at the least breath of wind move like one who blows the long hair of a girl. The great grace from which hope is born is the certainty of faith; the certainty of faith is the seed of the certainty of hope. The small seed that's planted today will only begin to come out in September of the coming year and only after four or five years does it begin to delineate itself as a little plant with those gentle and strange characteristics.

"To hope it is necessary to have received a great grace," the great grace of certainty in the present. No one has certainty in the present; everyone has certainty in the present when they're not thinking of it; if they think about it ... they have no certainty. Everyone has certainty when he or she isn't thinking of it – money, a political career, an academic career – but if you go there when they're eating cake or panettone (cake or panettone is the same, because if they put a little Grand Marnier on panettone and warm it up a little it turns into a cake that's out of this world. I'll give you a recipe!) and you question them, they have no true certainty with regard to the ultimate meaning of living.

It's certainty regarding the present; therefore of a meaning in the present that, in time, makes a place for a certainty regarding the future. There's a period that seems like uncertainty, because the shape of the future isn't yet delineated: you know the tamarisk plant, you take out the seed, you plant it in the ground ... who knows what thing will come out of there? Who knows what form it will take? To understand what form it will take, you must wait for time to pass.

"To hope it is necessary to have received a great grace." The great grace represents, assures, a present in which a strange seed is planted through which hope will flower tomorrow. "Our hope for days unending now blossoms with the dawn."[7] Also because, my friend, you are interested in what will happen to you tonight, but then, tonight goes away and there's tomorrow night, then that goes away and there's the night after tomorrow night, then that goes away and you are fifty years old, then the fifty years go away and you are seventy, then seventy goes away and you are ninety-eight years old ... I assure you that a person very rarely reaches ninety-eight, the majority of people don't even arrive at eighty-eight, and after there's the great grace of the glory of God, the great grace of the end.

Man lives the present and imagines the future, projecting the present on the future, and this either distracts from the present or makes it vague, or twists it, it becomes a little strange: the present in the future, who knows? What does the Christian life do instead? It makes you live in the present with great attention towards all the things of the present; and paying attention even to the sea in front of you, you spot on the sea's ultimate horizon a little point; and it isn't a ship that's moving off, but one that's coming towards you. It's destiny that's coming to you; and the day in which you become aware of that little point that is destiny that's about to arrive is a great day, as it was for Christopher Columbus: that day when he began to glimpse a little stretch of land was a great day.

## A possession that is already given

Let's add another observation. We said that hope is certainty regarding the future that is based on the certainty about a present. But a present is truly the present insofar as you possess it; therefore hope is certainty in the future that is based on a possession already given, because you don't give yourself the present, you receive it: "it's a great grace." Hope is certainty regarding the future that is based on the certainty of a possession that is already given; *possession*, therefore in strict relation, profoundly with your person; *already given*, that comes to you from another; you don't conquer it.

The comparison of John in chapter six is right. What was Peter, John, and Andrew's hope in Jesus based on? For them, Jesus was one whom they called "you," He was a Presence: when they woke up in the morning, numbed by sleeping out in the open and He had spent the whole night praying, John, Andrew, and Peter felt – I use an approximate word – they had to "feel" the belonging to that man, because they could base all their hope for the future on that man; it was that man, to whom they accepted to belong, who founded their certainty for the future.

Jesus's relatives, in the third chapter of Mark,[8] who went to get Jesus while He was speaking in the square, did so because people were saying "He's crazy," not recognizing anything in Him – they didn't possess Him, they weren't in union with Him, they weren't bound to Him; He wasn't bound to them, He was nothing for them; they didn't have Him, and thus they could place on Him no prospect for the future. Since they didn't have Him, they didn't belong to Him, they couldn't even base a prospect for their future on Him.

## Certainty of fulfillment

As it should be written in all houses of the Gruppo Adulto: "The one who began this good work in you [what is good work? It is living life within the tiny or great awareness of the relationship with Christ, of the relationship with God made man] … The one who began this good work in you [this great grace] will bring it to perfection until the day of Christ Jesus [will bring it to perfection at the end, on the day of destiny]."[9] To be sure that He will bring to perfection what He gave me means to be sure of my happiness, to be sure of my destiny, to be sure of my fulfillment, to be sure of the aim of life. What one needs to be sure of – if one isn't sure of this, everything breaks and crumbles – is one's own destiny, one's own happiness, of being saved. As it says then in the letter to the Philippians, chapter one: "The one who began this good work in you will bring it to perfection until the day of Christ Jesus." It's a word of hope, of hope in its true sense, thus of certainty. The way they use the word in dialect[10] isn't hope: *sperem*; Christian hope is certainty, a certainty with regard to the future instead of the present. "The one who began this good work in you will bring it to perfection until the day of Christ Jesus." It's a breath of fresh air because He gave it to you, it's evident He gave it to you, because you have it and you didn't give it to yourself; and if He is also the one who will bring it to fulfillment, you can all but rest assured! Rest, in fact, tranquil, in peace: *in ipsum et dormiam et requiescam*[11] [with Him, in peace, I sleep and rest]. You can sleep in peace because the future is sure; certainty for the future comes from a great grace. The great grace is present; certainty for the future derives from this present.

Up until now we've developed some reflections on what hope is: a certainty with regard to the future that can be based only on the certainty of something in the present, great and large, because it has to sustain the whole future. It rests on the present, and for you to have a sure present, on which you can base your whole future, is a great grace.

This afternoon we'll cover the second point; the third we'll deal with when God wills it; a war can break out, as in Sarajevo. Think, those of you who live in Ancona are two hundred kilometres from the point where people are massacred, and they live as if it's nothing. On the other hand, those whom they depend on to intervene, even if they're a little farther away because they live in Brussels or

London, not only sleep peacefully, but have parties and orgies, make horror films: they make more money.

## 2 THE DYNAMIC OF HOPE

What else can we say about hope? What else would you say about hope?

*Since nothing is automatic, how is hope born of faith? Is there a condition where, if one lives faith, hope is derived from it?*
The question is very correct and sharp. Since nothing automatic has human value – what does "nothing automatic" mean? Nothing that isn't free – how do you manage to affirm a certainty regarding tomorrow from faith in a present? It's very correct and very sharp as a question; I would like it to be understood before I give a response to it, as I see that you feel like being here as much as I do!

### Desire

What kind of movement must happen to arrive at a certainty regarding the future from a certainty of the present? It has to do with freedom; freedom has something to do with everything. But the word freedom, here, is important: in what sense does freedom have something to do with it?

*As desire, as a plea that lasts through something already begun …*
The dynamic of faith, which is to believe, to affirm a present that is exceptional in its power, becomes certainty for a future changing itself into definite desire satisfied by

faith itself, transforming itself into a plea to the power that faith reveals as present: "As an entreaty, as desire that brings to maturity something already begun," the gift that Christ makes of Himself to us, in the present. Freedom is within desire, and asks with certainty that our happiness come from Him.

A little group of people is chatting in a village square; someone passing by speaks with them and they say: "This man is marvellous." Faith is born as a recognition of an exceptional Presence. The experience of an exceptional Presence makes a *desire* that has to do with the future well up in the heart of man: the desire that that man stay on, the desire that that man straighten out his household matters, straighten out his crazy wife, straighten out his son ... any type of desire; it's the dynamism of faith, as the recognition of a Presence, under the impact of the needs of the heart which, on hearing that man speak, awaken in all their depth. Thus the encounter with that man brought forth desires in them, desires that that man can fulfill – they're sure that man can handle them. The dynamic of faith is the affirmation of an experience; hope is the desire for something that happens in the future.

The second step we're taking is to indicate the dynamism proper to hope. Hope is born of an affirmation. How is it born? As affirmation of the fulfillment of a desire; it is born as an affirmation of the fulfillment of a desire. Maybe it's not clear? Meeting a person one says: "Wow, I've found a great man! If he's a great man he should resolve this urgent problem: straighten out my son."

Faith as the affirmation of a great Presence; hope as an affirmation that resolves, an affirmation of a desire, in which the needs of the heart are determined. An encounter excites, solicits, reawakens the needs of the heart; one starts to desire because this has to do with a type of future; one begins to desire.

These desires will be satisfied, right or wrong? This is the point. These desires, made according to the needs of your heart, can surely be actuated, can have the capacity to uphold the reason for hope concerning certainty for the future, only to the degree that – it isn't easy to say! – one trusts the content of faith, only to the degree that one abandons oneself, trusts and abandons oneself to the Presence that faith has indicated.

The needs of the heart say that the object of the heart exists, it exists in the future, because man is destined to be happy, just, true. He's destined for this, but the certainty that this will happen cannot be sustained by our heart. The certainty that this will happen can be derived only from a Presence that faith recognizes, from an exceptional presence that faith recognizes. Only this can sustain the reason for a certainty in the future.

So it's a clarifying form. I repeat it; pay attention, tell me whether you understand what I say or not. The heart of man – we've studied it in *The Religious Sense*[12] – is made up of fundamental or ideal needs; thus it is impelled towards the future in the direction of those ideal needs; he cannot be sure they will be met, he cannot be sure of not betraying them, for example. He's impelled towards the future; the heart is impelled towards the future by the desire that these needs be fulfilled. When does this desire become certainty? How can this desire become certainty? This desire becomes certainty to the degree to which it attains confidence in the power of a great Presence. Thus the dynamic of hope is a desire that cannot last in time. It would be bitterly deluded, if it wasn't supported, supported as reason by faith, by the certainty in the power of a great Presence.

## The certainty of fulfillment

Let's take another step. How does the heart, how does hope (certainty for the future derived from trust in the great Presence), how does this desire for actuation of the good, which attains confidence in the certainty of the great Presence, become certainty that the great Presence will respond?

Hope, as a need that carries out that which the heart desires, cannot be certainty that is born of that same heart, because the heart doesn't know, it desires but it doesn't know. How can it become certainty of the heart – and therefore hope in the Christian sense of the word – certainty that carries out that which the heart humanly desires? The nature of the dynamic of hope is desire but it's a desire that cannot be sure of itself; how can it become sure of itself?

*Because He promised it to me.*
Desire becomes sure of itself when it asks, when it asks, when the desire of the heart becomes a plea. And the plea is sustained by a certainty in the response that the great Presence gives, because the great Presence has promised it.

"Ask," this was the word. But "has promised it to me" is fundamental, it is what makes the entreaty itself certain according to reason. Even if the promise is already implied in the fact that the great Presence exists.

## The dream and the ideal

Let's add an observation, which is a *nota bene*. The needs of the heart demand to be fulfilled; since man doesn't have the strength to fulfill them, to reach the objective that they make him foresee, man gives form to this claim according to a vision, according to the fragile and ultimately illusory substance that is called a dream. Man's heart dreams, so that its needs be satisfied: it dreams, gives a positive form to its path. But the dream of man's heart can't sustain the reasons for certainty, for the certainty that the needs be fulfilled. Such certainty that these be fulfilled comes from the fact that the great Presence *promised* that man would be fulfilled, if man were to ask Him. Therefore, from memory, hope exalts the promise (covenant, as Holy Mass says); from faith, hope exalts the promise.

The great Presence gave the promise, gives the promise that, insofar as one asks, it will be fulfilled. Here is freedom; man's freedom in front of his destiny is a question, which is the position of the beggar or of the poor. The object of certainty that the needs of the heart will be fulfilled is called the ideal. The needs of the heart rest their certainty on their plea to the great Presence.

To understand hope, therefore, it is very important to distinguish between the dream and the ideal. The dream arises because the needs of the heart, the original needs, crave fulfillment so deeply that, forgetting the great Presence, they tend to imagine for themselves the form that will fulfill them. This form always takes as its starting point a not-great presence, a presence that is not great. It's not that I'm confused, it's that in these things it's necessary to be on the lookout for a way of putting things more simply.

Man's heart craves happiness. If he lives the faith, then it is certain that this happiness will be given to him by the great Presence, because the great Presence has promised it. He has promised it to the point of dying to allow it.

I have said:

- the needs of the heart are needs for happiness;
- without faith, this certainty of happiness cannot be reasonable, but acquires a form, a form that is given by the heart itself, taking as a pretext some presence that still isn't the great Presence (man for woman, a baby for a mother, money for the one who loves money, political success for one involved in politics) and this is called a dream; man's heart is tempted by dreams;
- instead, man's heart is made for happiness. If it recognizes the great Presence, if it lives the certainty of the great Presence, it understands that the reason for the certainty that its desires will be fulfilled can be found in the great Presence; therefore ask with the help of the great Presence to reach them in the way that He gave them an eternal form: this form is called the ideal. Thus, hope is either translated into desire for a dream or in the ideal desire.

Now, when we have the retreat we'll even remedy the way of saying all this, but even said in this manner it doesn't strike me as obscure. Let's take another step now.

*I haven't understood what the ideal is.*
The ideal is the object of perfection, of happiness for which the heart of man is made, that he cannot realize alone; alone he can give it a dreamy form, because he takes as his starting point circumstances and not the great Presence. The ideal, instead, is the heart's desire for happiness, which it recognizes as possible only with the help of the great Presence. The ideal, therefore, is the ultimate desire of the heart, which man tries to reach trusting the great Presence. This difference between the dream and the ideal is very important.

## A question that imbues everything

If that which should prevail is the ideal and not the dream, the need for the happiness of man's heart will be realized according to the form that the mystery of the great Presence establishes; and this form is none other than the great Presence Himself; the form is Christ Himself; it's the mystery of God, that for which man is made.

Now you understand well that all the circumstances in which man lives are temptations to dream or signs of the ideal. What does a sign of the ideal mean? It means that man understands that the attractiveness of all circumstances is something temporary that refers him back to the definitive and ultimate attraction of the great Presence. It means that all circumstances, even if they're good, beautiful, and fascinating, recall the unsurpassable beauty of the presence of the Mystery, of the presence of Christ.

Therefore the desire, which represents the essence of hope, is that Christ comes; that, even in the temporary circumstances, one comes closer to Christ, that Christ be more glorified, or (and it's the same) Christ comes, or (and it's the same) that Christ reveals Himself in what we do. Thus the form of hope is given by the last word in the Bible: "Come, Lord Jesus." This question must imbue everything, especially in its most correct and difficult formula, most beautiful and difficult, analogous to Peter's response to Christ: "Lord, make me love you."[13] Therefore, going through the day, what one ultimately asks is only this: that the love for Christ increase, so that man may walk towards his happiness.

Concluding, we can say that hope is the first characteristic of an I, of a person who walks in time, and thus hope sheds light on whether what happens – that is, circumstances – drives man to disappointment, cheats man of his freedom to ask, or reveals the great Presence that he has met and that becomes the indicated destiny of all things, that content of which all things become a sign, and above all the ultimate object of his plea.

## 3  TOWARDS THE POSSESSION OF AN ARDUOUS GOOD

I drink the beer they have put here for me. Thanks to whoever had the nice thought to give me beer ... I can't give you any, there's too little!

When Vera or Mandy sing out the first notes of a new song they're like the cultivators of evangelical memory, who cast the seeds on the hard earth, because it hasn't been well ploughed – in the sense of being prepared to learn to sing – but the seed is cast anyway and, after one time, two times, three times, four times, the seed starts to take root, even if somewhat weakly, so that you need to work the hoe to get in deeper; but at a certain point, for better or worse, the song is there.

So, when we speak our words to you, that were spoken to us just as they are to you, we remember the time in which even for us these words were like stones that were cast in our face: we didn't penetrate them, nor did they penetrate us. But the mercy of the Lord lies precisely in the patience with which you repeat things in time; we are made to repeat things in time; repeating and repeating, feeling the hail on the head and then another fall of hail and then still another, until finally these words penetrate our brain, until they begin to penetrate the heart. First they penetrate the brain, and therefore they still mean almost nothing, but then they penetrate the heart and now they begin to mean something.

So what is the first consequence of what I'm saying? We shouldn't marvel at it if we don't understand, but woe to anyone who, not understanding, gives up there, and says, "I don't understand." Watch that person! It's all over for that person; it's a refusal that will always be without fruit. Instead you must repeat them or – as the Bishop said this morning at the big meeting of the Compagnia delle Opere[14] [Company of Works] – you must look values in the face.

A word that is meant to indicate a piece of our life is called a value; not a piece in the chronological sense, not a piece in the anatomical sense, but a piece in the living sense of the term "life," a piece of the I that is walking towards its destiny. You must look it in the face, you must get used to looking these words in the face; even only having the word there in front of your eyes and looking at it, a little or a lot, allows you to be penetrated by it. If you look at it then it's also a plea to God at the same time: "Lord, make me understand this word." Then the response comes more quickly and you are able to understand more quickly the greatness of certain terms – greatness because they embrace life – and the satisfaction of the heart that certain terms provoke, produce: the joy they produce, because there is no spring of joy if not the truth of words that are repeated to indicate something true, alive, and conclusive.

Certainty and desire

Up to now what have we said about hope? First, we said that hope is certainty of the future motivated by certainty in the present; and, second, that the dynamic that hope imprints on our I, on our conscience, is called desire.

Why do you write these things down? You should have them already written down. Watch out if you're waiting for the mimeographs; first, because they never arrive on time, and second because, if you unload the certainty of the words that are said on the fact that you have a mimeograph, it's as if you tried to be like Dante Alighieri because you have a copy of the *Divine Comedy*, do you know what I mean? Instead it's because of that which vibrates in you, that is regenerated in you, that you become able to repeat, to comment, to feel, to feel again.

Now: hope as certainty for the future; it's the dynamic of such certainty that is desire. The certainty of a good that is still absent, that will come in the future; therefore a waiting, consciously; therefore, a desire.

## The desire for an arduous good

Certainty regarding a future good, not a present one, resting on a certainty that is present, and that expresses itself as desire regarding a good, an *arduous*[15] value, said Saint Thomas Aquinas. What does a good or a value that is desired, but is arduous, mean? That one desires a good or a value, and having it carries a price. In some way it costs you something, it's arduous, it's toilsome, it exacts pain and effort.

## The inevitable uncertainty

The first thing to note is a kind of premise to what we have to say: between the certainty of faith and the seed that this certainty of faith is for future certainty, there's a period that can seem like uncertainty. Uncertainty in what sense? In the sense that the picture of this future still isn't delineated: "Who knows how it will be?" Hell? No! Not hell. Why not hell? Maybe because hell doesn't exist? Because hell isn't an object of hope!

The picture of the future still isn't delineated and so the "who knows how it will be?" hangs like a cloud over the relationship between certainty in the present and impetus towards the future, future desire, like a weight, a weight of uncertainty. Between certainty of faith and certainty of hope that is born of faith, there is still an atmosphere in the beginning, a moment, a passage of uncertainty that isn't true uncertainty, because otherwise it wouldn't be certainty any longer; and if it isn't certainty any longer, it isn't hope any longer. Instead no, certainty of faith generates certainty of hope, but the manner in which this certainty of hope is drawn out in us leaves a kind of disorientation, leaves a kind of tribulation, a kind of doubt that isn't doubt, that is uncertainty, because you aren't able to imagine, to delineate in any way what this future will be like.

For example, one of the aspects for which the memory of Christ is so weak in many moments of our life is a kind of uncertainty regarding Him, that isn't uncertainty regarding Him, otherwise it would be a lack of faith, but it's a difficulty in delineating within ourselves how this all happened. For example, Jesus, who brings the widow of Nain's son back to life: it's by putting ourselves within that moment that that moment becomes a factor of relief, a factor of joy, a factor of ever deeper persuasion in us. For this we can always go back to the first chapter of Saint John, when Andrew and John went to Jesus for the first time: the first two who saw Him, for the first time, in a certain way. They went there, they were there watching Him speak ... and we aren't able to imagine how it must have been. You understand very well that those two were struck by the exceptionality of that man, and in fact we say that they *watched* Him speak because they didn't understand what He said, and even we can't understand what He might have said to us. It's a kind of puzzlement, a feeling of doubt or of uncertainty regarding the whole picture; we aren't able to imagine it well, to re-imagine and picture the whole thing. It leaves a kind of trembling feeling.

It can't be that the difficulty in imagining ourselves, in delineating how this future can be, becomes a reason for doubt regarding the future. It would be irrational if we weren't certain of the future, only because we aren't able to imagine it, to delineate how this picture of the future can be. Sure, if it's in the future, we still haven't experienced it, we can't know how it is! But that it is depends on the certainty of faith. We are sure that it's there but we aren't sure of how to think of it, of how to delineate the picture of the future.

But this is also an advantage, because we can vent ourselves in many ways, according to temperament, according to fantasy. The first time I read to you about John and Andrew[16], you had never imagined what I was trying to say. But if you were attentive, after, even you began to think about it like that and you began to learn to imagine even other passages of the gospel that way; for example, the sinner who, weeping, kisses Jesus' feet,[17] Zaccheus curled up in the tree, who hears "Zaccheus" from Him who is passing by.[18]

The difficulty in delineating how this future will be is not an obstacle to the certainty of the future. The difficulty in delineating how paradise will be doesn't affect it, doesn't invalidate certainty regarding paradise; the reason of paradise is totally different from the capacity we have to imagine paradise. It has to do with reason and not with images. Now an image is worth nothing? No! An image helps reason, when you know how to use it. An image is helpful, it's a little servant who runs to get the chestnuts or runs to get the glass of beer, you know what I mean? It doesn't have dignity, the consistency of reason; it isn't the master. I insist upon this because, in my opinion, much of our emptiness, much of our fear, much of our disinterest arises because we confuse the incapacity that we have to imagine the future with certainty regarding this future: certainty is the object of reason; the delineation of what this future will be like is an imaginative capacity that some have more of, others less.

So up until now I wanted to remove the veil of a useless objection: confusing imagination and fantasy with reason. Certainty is the object of reason; better, it's based on reason, not on imagination; and the vagueness of imagination doesn't give us any motive to doubt reason.

*a) A difficult path*
The first point of a meditative development of the word hope inasmuch as dynamic certainty reaches out to possess an *arduous* good: the fulfillment of our destiny always implies a difficult path, because the fulfillment of destiny, the path to destiny, is a trial. Trial in Latin would be exam: it's an exam, a trial. The path to destiny always involves an effort because the path is a trial to be overcome: in this sense you say that it's arduous. Crossing a high river is arduous, climbing to the top of Mont Blanc is arduous: every trial is arduous, every trial has a little of this adjective

within it. How do you say exam in Latin? *Periculum*, it's a danger, therefore a trial; *pericolo* doesn't mean danger, it means a trial.

## b) The strength of Jesus

Second idea. The supremely important thing is that the strength of that present reality, which is called Jesus, the strength of Jesus will never abandon us and is stronger than any difficulty or effort.

"I love you, God my strength,"[19] says a psalm with a phrase that is repeated as an antiphon, "I love you, God my strength," or as Saint Paul said: "I have the strength for everything [*omnia possum*, I can do anything] through Him who empowers me [*in Eo qui me confortat*, in He who comforts me]."[20] Not in the sense that He tells me "Dear one, dear one, courage"; *confortat* means "I have strength with Him," together with Him I have strength. To comfort ultimately means exactly this, otherwise what comfort would there be? They're cutting your head off, the new Jacobins, and somebody comes over to "comfort you": "Oh, don't worry about it; oh, don't worry."

The famous phrase of the last of Jesus's discourses in Saint John: "I will not leave you orphans, I will return to you, I will leave you my Spirit:"[21] Leave you my spirit means I leave you myself; the Spirit of Christ is his I, it's the energy of his I. "I will be so present as to place continually within you, to provide within you my energy and my strength." The Spirit, then, indicates the way in which the great Presence travels the path with us; the Spirit is the energy of light and of heart with which Christ maintains

His presence and thus helps us, comforts us, in confronting all our trials.

In what way does He help us? In what sense is the Spirit a light? *First*, He makes us understand that it isn't trials that define life, life isn't fulfilled in trials; but, *second*, through trials – a trial is a "through" – He makes us walk, thus building our life, our life that won't ever fail. To construct it's necessary to make an effort, even if it isn't the effort that fulfills the aim: the builder's sense of work isn't the effort he makes, but, through that effort, he builds the house and takes home his pay on the 27th of the month, as long as the company doesn't go bankrupt in the meantime! *Third*, but above all, the Spirit of Christ, always present on the path through all our trials, teaches us the great word on the road of hope: patience.

*A corollary: patience.* "In your patience you will possess life," says Jesus in the holy gospel;[22] patience being the capacity to carry – *patior* means to carry, to carry on one's shoulders – being ultimately the capacity to carry everything, in us and in reality, to carry all the circumstances, carry everything with the reasonable courage of not rejecting anything. Why have we said *reasonable* courage? Because reason is consciousness of reality according to the totality of its factors – all the explanations that are given for reason miss the value of reason, because in order to explain, they are forced to forget or reject something, said the first volume of the School of Community.[23] Whoever is forced to explain, to reject, or to forget something isn't reasonable. Reason must explain everything. Patience is the capacity to carry everything with the reasonable courage to not reject anything, to not forget anything and – watch out! – to not refute anything. They are three important words.

*To reject*: Like babies to whom you say: "Look, what a beautiful apple!" and they say, "No!" because they're fooling around – to reject what is evident, regarding the evident.

*To forget*: Regarding the fact that something doesn't interest you in the moment, or to sustain a certain position, or because we have a interest in forgetting it. Forgetting is to avoid, avoid.

*To refute*: When you understand something, you understand its importance, you understand its necessity, but you spit it out.

You should read the New Testament, especially the letter to the Romans, above all chapters 5 and 8, the letter of Saint Peter and the letter of James, the first chapter. But you must read everything, looking for the word patience; every time the word patience shows up you'll learn something of its value.

Do you remember Atlas, from antiquity, the giant who carried the world? Patience is much more than "Atlas" who carries the world. That was a stoic image, a presumption of stoic magnanimity, a presumption because man doesn't carry the world; if he tries, the world, at a certain point, crushes him. This is the most dignified philosophy in the world: that of stoic Atlas. In *The Religious Sense* you have an example of this stoicism that doesn't fulfill its aim: the example of little Herr Friedmann.[24] Because in front of the weight of things – think of death, everything ends – what has man thought in all times? Two things: let's forget and let's enjoy life, tomorrow we'll die and now let's enjoy life; or instead, if they were serious, had a minimum of seriousness – that is a greater zest than the stupidity of pure pleasure – the stoic formula: bear things on your shoulders; magnanimity, as they call it now, bearing on your shoulders. But one who takes the world on his shoulders takes a step and the world crushes him, he can't support this kind of weight, alone.

"In your patience you will possess life," says Jesus. Think of the proximity between this bearing life and being crushed by life in the sense of being crucified, for example, in the sense of enduring: to carry and endure, humanly speaking, are like two parallel lines, two parallel roads.

### c) Faithfulness to belonging

Third point. What does the effort of hope, which is the fabric of patience, consist of? The effort of hope is to remain. "Remain in me." Read the fourteenth and fifteenth chapters of Saint John: "Remain in me." Persist in remaining in Christ, in faithfulness to belonging, faithfulness to one's own life as a belonging, as a recognized belonging.

But is this belonging like a baby invisible in its mother's womb? Faithfulness to belonging, which is the fabric of patience or the toil of hope, has a way of expressing itself. What is it? Asking; it's asking or, better still – since it isn't one's asking that he is one thing and he wants something else, but it's asking for everything – it's begging. Asking or begging of Christ present. Go and read the two pages of the gospel: Luke 11:1–11 and Luke 18:1–8. If one reads them with faith and attention one can no longer doubt and no longer be afraid. Read slowly, look these passages well in the face, make yourselves aware that there isn't anything in the world that you can attribute all these things to, nothing in the world, no one: not a father, not a mother, not even the best mother and the best father, the most intelligent. Man would be totally abandoned if he didn't abandon himself to this belonging.

The enemies of this faithfulness in belonging, the most notable enemies, are first, discontinuity – in psychology, this neurosis is called cyclothymia: one day up, one day down, in the evening up, in the morning down. A schizophrenic is one who is broken from head to toe; discontinuity is more a variation in mood: one time he has his nose in the air and the next time he laughs immoderately; and you don't know how to take him; you see that he laughs and you laugh too, but then ... so the discontinuity. And then, the toil and the pain.

### d) Forgiveness

Fourth point. What is the most acute aspect of this toil? What is the most difficult aspect of this faithfulness to begging and to asking? What is the most acute aspect of the toil that we've pointed out before, the toil of hope? Forgiveness; asking for forgiveness, certain of being forgiven; the taking up again after the mistake, not because we're able to remedy the situation, but because, asking Christ present with His Spirit, begging pardon of Him, it's as if the mistake we've made were to disappear and become strength in us, a desire to please Him. "Simon, do you love me?" not: "You got on my nerves, you betrayed me." No, no, no, he had done that or betrayed Him so many times, but: "Do you love me?"

To take up hope once again after one of our errors is such a great gesture that the poet Péguy defines it as "the secret mystery of hope,"[25] because pardon of evil is a mystery in itself. "The secret mystery of hope that with bad water makes pure water and makes fresh souls out of old souls." It's rebirth. Baptism is the beginning of this rebirth, a principle that operates for one hundred years if someone lives for a hundred years, for 103 if someone lives for 103 years, that operates 1,299 times if one has committed 1,299 sins and 10,003 times if one has committed 10,003 sins.

## The opposite of patience

But as a more important observation, which Péguy himself makes, there is the possibility in us for the opposite of patience. The opposite of patience isn't impatience: impatience is a limit of patience. The opposite of patience is that species of worm-filled resignation – like the worms that turn slowly, slowly – it's that twisted proceeding, it's that stretching of one's arms and legs uselessly, that comes from so many things, for example from laziness. But laziness doesn't define anything, it's just a person's attitude, from which, sooner or later, something very ugly emerges. It's called lukewarmness. Lukewarmness is to follow the road of hope with your nose out of joint, your head twisted, exactly as a worm twists in order to walk; and whoever is here without being here and therefore isn't pleasing to God "neither to God nor to his enemies" (he can't be pleasing to God and he wouldn't be pleasing to Satan either, if Satan didn't wait for the moment to eat him up, everything!). But above all luke-warmness is a way of living the following of Christ where you bore yourself, we bore ourselves, that is without light, without brilliance, without creative energy, without sweet-ness, without a plan – therefore without hope! To hope without hoping, which is the opposite of that great phrase that Saint Paul said of Abraham: "Hoping against every hope."[26] Lukewarmness is the opposite of strength.

## Witness

One final *nota bene*. The greatest trial of life, therefore of hope, on the path of hope, would be death – if Christ hadn't been resurrected. Man had nothing more to fear from death from the moment Christ rose from the dead, even as far as reaching a point of such intensity of hope that he would desire to die for Christ.

Witness – we'll conclude this way – is a little piece of death for Christ, every witness. It's concretely called mis-sion: life as mission, going away, *partir c'est un peu mourir*, that all in all is mission, but mission is the aim of life. In fact, what was the aim of the life of Christ? To save the world, save every one of us, save me and you. Therefore Christ Himself said that He waited for the trial of His death with a longing desire, a pining desire, when He spoke of the bloodbath and of how He desired that it come about. Because death is nothing more than the culmination of the trial, whose aim cannot be other than the witness of accepting the Mystery of God.

In *The Religious Sense* read attentively the chapter that speaks of the two factors that comprise the experience of the I.[27] Read the School of Community again from the beginning, otherwise you won't understand anything we're offering you, and instead of seeds in open turf, the things we're saying to you will be like stones thrown in your face.

## HOPE: ASSEMBLY

*Oh! doux pays de Chanaan* (Oh! Sweet Land of Canaan) is the song of hope.[28] All of the themes of hope that we touched on are here: the trial, the toil, the reasons you must have to be able to perform the toil worthy of a man; it's the arduous future. A people on a journey in the desert, who don't know where they will settle down, know neither the road nor anything else. What is the strength that this people had that enabled them to journey forty years towards a destiny that they didn't know?

*God was with them.*
God was with them – the strength was God with them, the strength of God with them was called the Covenant. In what form were the terms of hope made known to them? As a promise.

*Man's heart is a promise*
Let's take man – all men and women and us as such. What is life's destiny (because the journey is life)? That is to say:

what is the content of the promise? How do you know this destiny? The heart of man. Man is born with this heart; that is, born with this hope; man is born with a heart in which lies a promise; is born with a heart that you can define only as a promise. The core of life is a promise. And this is why one must re-establish oneself in action every day, put oneself in action again.

How did He make this promise to the Hebrew people? When did the promise of God begin?

*With Abraham.*
With Abraham – He told him: "I promise you that..." Read the fifteenth chapter of Genesis, when Abraham walks, walks, walks, and one evening under the starry sky he says: "Lord, nothing's coming to a conclusion here except for my life. I'm not reaching what you promised me – you had promised me to be the leader of a great people, and here, my life's passing by, life's growing short" [as a bishop who was very sick told me when I went to visit him; as soon as he sat down, he told me: "Life's growing short"]. Just like this, Abraham, who was already over a hundred, even he seems to say: "Life's growing short, so where is what you promised me? I don't even have one child and my heir can't be anyone other than the head of my servants: Eliezer."[29] This is where Abraham is put to the test, his first serious test.

So what does the Lord do? He does nothing but repeat his promise to him; he leads him out from the tent, makes him look at the sky and says: "Count the stars if you can: your descendants will be as great as these"; nothing else – he repeats his promise. God can't do less than His word;

therefore, He needs nothing else to reassure man. In fact, the faith of Abraham is that he believed in the word of God, he abandoned himself to the word of God. It is in that chapter that the fulfillment of the covenant occurs, the renewal of the promise.

The Covenant is the tangible, physical, experiential expression of the promise of God to Abraham. The last half of this chapter is one of the most striking in all of world literature, when God reveals Himself as a firebrand.

Abraham's hope is reasonable. Why? First, what does it mean that Abraham's hope in God's Covenant with him is reasonable? Abraham's hope is reasonable – that is, the certainty that the future would fulfill what God had promised – because He who made the promise was God and God cannot deceive. God's promise corresponded to Abraham's heart and the promise was made by God. For these two reasons, it was reasonable.

Thus, the life that is given to us is hope, reasonable hope, hope that is reasonably founded. Why? Because it comes to us from God – we didn't make ourselves – and we feel what God made us for in our hearts, it corresponds to our hearts. Just as Abraham felt the burden of being put to the test, so much so that he complained – the fifteenth chapter is Abraham's complaint – so do we feel many times in life like reviving this complaint: "I don't have this, I don't have that. Who knows?" The true complaint is normally expressed like a shadow that extends across the expanse of the spirit: "Who knows?." But it's unjust. Why is it unjust?

*Because it censures something that has already happened to us.*
It censures something that has already happened to you. What has already happened to you? What's happened is that you have been made with a heart like this, with a heart that has a need for happiness. What has already happened to you is that you were created and therefore what you feel is divine because it derives from Him who made you.

But what we have said up until now is valid for all men – valid for Christians and valid also for the pagan, for the most pagan man in the centre of Africa, for the Pygmies. The Pygmies are a tribe that retreated, little by little, as people arrived on African territory. Retreating, retreating, they locked themselves in hard-to-reach territories where others had no desire to go; they stayed in these almost inaccessible territories and they didn't develop socially because they cut off all their contacts, all the relationships with those that had come, that they had considered a danger.

Both for the Pygmies in Africa and for me, everything we have said is equally valid, and this is the first incredibly beautiful thing that the religious phenomenon establishes in the world. It's the first common reference for men and women: what our nature is straining towards can be perceived and attained in the same way by all. What we have said up to this point holds for everyone. So what's the difference?

*That I was chosen.*
Let's put a hold on the word *chosen*; suspend it because it comes later. *Chosen* is what distinguishes me from a Pygmy.

*An encounter happened to me.*

Something happened to us that didn't happen to others. But why did it happen?

What we have said up until now is valid for all; but for all men and women, what we have said up until now, which we've repeated in such a simple way, which seems so clear, is not clear. It's not clear for all.

Think about the images with which everyone covers the mystery of their future: the images with which the Bantus of Africa cover it, or the images with which the Buddhists of India, China, or Japan cover it. These images are, if you wish, only ideas, but ultimately they are true images. In the face of our common destiny – which should be a source of fresh air and security, even in the midst of the whole trial of life – we all seem incapable of standing firm. And the real attitude with which we stand in front of our destiny is like an ultimate – I don't know how to say it – an ultimate reserve, almost cautiously, an ultimate reserve or, as we said earlier, a big "Who knows?"

When people are together in a Hindu temple or in a temple of the gods with a wizard – when they are together, they say things that their religion says, and this is ultimately positive in respect to destiny – it's more or less positive. But then, they, in defining their destiny, must also define the fact that man goes against his destiny (he betrays it many times); that is, that destiny rewards or punishes. Therefore, a tangle of images to explain one thing and another; when they are together, they affirm, but when they are alone, when they look with sincerity at their life, "Who knows?" is the general attitude.

So on the one hand, there is something positive with respect to the answer to the heart, of their being created. This positive thing assumes many guises, it hides the answer behind many different images. On the other hand, while this becomes a peremptory matter, a constitutive matter of their traditional rites, in the privacy of their lives, in the consciousness of their daily lives, "Who knows?" prevails, even without their realizing it. And then – third – they don't have an answer to the problem of evil, a clear answer to the problem of evil. If they make a mistake, if they resist – and life is full of this resistance – what will happen, how do they bring back their security? So, one sits oneself down, puts one's head in one's hands and says: "Mmm, who knows?"

To men of all ages who sat with their head in their hands saying "Who knows?" a thought came into their hearts ...

Maybe I've recounted this story in *The Religious Sense*. I read a big book about a French missionary explorer named Delafosse, who stayed with the African Pygmies; he lived more than twenty years – who knows how he did it, twenty years! – in the midst of those Pygmies to study them. And after twenty years, he published four large volumes in which he describes their ultimate philosophy of life.[30] And their ultimate philosophy is similar to Aristotle's: the maximum of the evolution of thought and the minimum affirmation of thought have equal frameworks. However Delafosse thought them to be polytheistic because they had many images of gods, many idols. At a certain point, after having been with them for many years, he realized from certain phrases that it was simplistic to call them idol-worshipers. He dug deep and discovered that they had a distinct idea of a supreme entity, of a unique being, about whom they didn't know how to say more, because – they gave him this explanation – their fathers had invoked this god, but, at a certain point, he hadn't answered any more; he went hunting and he no longer heard man's cries. They kept crying out for many years; many, many years. But he didn't hear them, he was always hunting! He was always hunting and no longer heard them. And then, they said to Delafosse: "You see, for that reason, we couldn't run back to the idols," to something lesser, but stronger than themselves. What was inevitable was the recognition that they could only live for the relationship with something greater than themselves. Ultimately, this was one, a unique entity, to whom they didn't pay tribute with prayer, because he didn't listen to them anymore. And so they turned to subsidiary gods who were at the level of their daily lives: gods that could understand their daily problems.

In the history of religions, particularly for the studies done by Eliade,[31] this has become the prevalent opinion of the more serious scholars (one is our personal friend, Father Ries).[32]

Anyway, from his way of conceiving of God, from his way of conceiving of the force on which he depends and from his way of conceiving of the destiny for which he was made, from all that, man derives the image of daily life and of the man-woman relationship, of the relationship of the people in the village, of the tribe, the concept of the past and the concept of the future. How he treats human beings and things, how he conceives of relationships, derives from how he imagines the force on which he depends and the destiny towards which he is going. Regarding this, read the first two chapters of the letter to the Romans of Saint Paul, and then read the seventeenth chapter of the Acts of the Apostles, where it speaks of Saint Paul in the Areopagus of Athens, where all the philosophers, the thinkers of that time, gathered to discuss freely (something that in modern nations isn't possible – not only in the Communist ones – because if you express an opinion different from today's television, the day after, you're attacked as a being who is out of line). So, I was saying, that the way to conceive of relationships sprung from how they conceived of the ultimate dependence, from how they conceived of ultimate dependence. Therefore, a great aberration, it wasn't possible for them to maintain a natural relationship in a correct position. All natural relationships – with themselves, with men, with things (the majority hadn't even thought of relationships with themselves) – were somehow altered, they couldn't stand on their own.

Because of this, there has always been in the history of man – as I was saying before – someone, some bizarre spirit, or better, some more enlightened spirit, who thought: "If the Mystery that made us, if the God that created us – if this God that is completely mute, that we don't even pray to any more – would come and make Himself seen, would make Himself known! The only way to know Him is for Him to come and make Himself known because we, with all of our efforts, aren't able to conceive of Him." There was a great man, like a piece of gold in the world's desert, in the desert of the path that people had to travel. Who was this figure in the journey of the Jews? Melchizedek – he's also in the Mass. Melchizedek, having fallen in with Abraham, recognized by instinct, that is, by God's suggestion, that Abraham was sent by God.[33] And Abraham respects Melchizedek because Melchizedek had had the intuition that man depends on the one God in order to know Him and to be able to serve Him with a dignified life. Or else, another name, in pagan circles, closer to us: Plato, in *Phaedo*,[34] four centuries before Christ; four centuries before Christ means shortly after the prophet Isaiah. And in this sense, the Hebrew people, the descendants of Abraham, showed their superiority with respect to all the other peoples; because the people that came after Abraham had a succession of prophets and religious geniuses that spoke of the ultimate God and of the ultimate destiny with a coherence that lasted for centuries and centuries and centuries, up until the second half of the second century before Christ. There's even a psalm that says: "There are no more prophets among us"[35]; in an age when the Jews thought they had to re-establish their freedom with their own effort. The great history of the Maccabees can be read in a book, a Norwegian novel by Pär Lagerkvist entitled *Herod and Mariamne*.[36]

But when God came, who recognized Him? He was recognized by the people who, in the face of what is arduous, behaved as we described last time. The Jews who were living with feelings of humility, of trust in God, of abandon to God, of continuing certainty even with their trials; those who lived thus, recognized Him. So much so that some who lived thus even went so far at a certain point – to wait for him – as to live in the temple, like old Simeon, Anna the prophetess ... or the Christmas shepherds; or think about the spirit of Saint Joseph, but even before that, about the spirit with which Mary lived.

Those who had those sentiments recognized Him; those who didn't have them, did not even recognize Him when he raised Lazarus, who had been dead for four days, from the dead. "Some, seeing this, believed in Him, but others ran ahead to Jerusalem in order to accuse Him, through the Jews."[37]

Therefore, the big question is to return to being little children[38] – "If you will not be like little children ..." – the big question is to return to the origin, the big question is to return to how God made us. Really, what is morality? Morality is to live with the attitude in which God made us. Only he who has this attitude recognizes His Presence. Read the eleventh chapter of Saint Matthew, verses 25–27.

All of the apostles were like this, save one who followed him – he was like all the others; moreover, he was full of initiative, so much so that Jesus put him in charge of the purse. He made him the administrator of the group. But he didn't follow Him with those sentiments – he was hoping for something else. The apostles also were hoping for something else, they were hoping that Jesus would finally bring the Kingdom of Israel, the Kingdom of the Hebrew people, to dominate the world and their ministries of this world; but – even if they had the mentality of everyone with these images – there was an attachment to Jesus that was sharper than these images to which they had remained faithful. This is so true that when the risen Jesus encounters them for the first time, they say: "Master, so now you'll establish the Kingdom of Israel?" as if He weren't dead, as if nothing had happened; they follow the mentality of everyone else. And Jesus quietly says: "It's not like that! The time of these events is known only by the Father."[39] And they are so childlike near Jesus, they let it drop; they don't hold to the demand that He answer their questions just as they may have imagined, but they remain attached to Him more deeply than they were attached to their opinions, with a greater simplicity. Because being attached to one's own opinion requires the loss of simplicity, the introduction of a presumption and the predominance of one's own imagination over the expectancy. This is precisely the great danger that all of us risk: the predominance of our images over the expectancy that God has awakened in our hearts and that Christ has renewed – no, more than that, that He has made precise. How did He make it precise? He made it precise by a relationship with Him: "Trust in me." Therefore, trust in the Mystery that made the world becomes daily trust; normal, a friendly trust with someone in the companionship, with Him.

But the predominance of one's own imagination is truly the one big temptation against faith in Jesus, therefore against obedience to God, against the plan of God, of which Jesus is the revealer, the messenger, the supreme exponent. Even in us, even in us, who have known the Lord – as the Angelus says, "that we to whom the incarnation of Christ Thy Son was made known by the message of an angel, may by His passion and cross" – even in us who, through Him, have known the road, who have known the conditions of the road, the direction of the road, the virtue of hope can be overcome by attachment to our images of the path and of destiny. Then, we complain when things don't happen as we want.

But a life that abandons itself to the force of destiny that is revealed in Christ, that abandons itself to the force of Christ, is a life where gladness dominates. "Be glad, I will come back to tell it to you again."[40] Or what Jesus says at the Last Supper, in the last discourse: "I told you all these things, so that my joy may be in you and your joy may be complete."[41]

The alternative to this, to the degree that this abandonment and certainty don't exist, is complaint. But it's not complaint that tears at the heart of a child who is suffering, it's complaint that stops up the heart and ears of he who is listening, it makes the lives of all who surround him burdensome and our life remains a condemnation for others, even for others. Life is full of complaining, life-complaint, that knows neither gladness nor, even less, the joy that stems from gladness.

And as he doesn't know gladness, I think that one who complains, who builds his life on complaints, doesn't know – among all the sentiments – tenderness. In relationships, tenderness is profoundly lacking. They can be in love as much as they want, but tenderness is lacking. There's a thrill that can seem to be tenderness, but it isn't tenderness because, first, it's temporary, and second, it's selfishness, self-centredness.

This twosome of gladness and tenderness – because only a glad heart can be tender in a relationship; tenderness is a sensitivity towards the joy of the other, a sensitivity that is attuned to wish and affirm the joy of the other – exists only in one who depends, accepts, is a child in front of Christ, like the apostles.

There are certain pages of the Gospel that are even more meaningful: the centurion wasn't one of His disciples, but go read about the centurion when he doesn't want Christ to go to his house because he is a captain and if he says to a soldier: "Go," that soldier goes; "Come," and he comes. And it's not necessary that he go where the soldier has to go, but the soldier obeys him, so much so that Jesus says: "I haven't found as much faith, not even in Israel [there's no adult in the people of God who maintained this faith, that is, this abandon and this awe at the greatness of God]."[42] There are many characters who aren't apostles who have this childlike simplicity in front of Christ. These are people capable of gladness in the heart and tenderness in relationships; and actually, that centurion was extremely tender, all of his concern was for a slave, he was tender towards a slave.

But now, I've answered for my part the question that I had; now you ask the questions.

Question. Question about what? About Martin Luther? Let's see if our concept of hope has become an image for you. It is a concept that becomes an image. Even if a concept comes unconsciously from an image, that is, from an impression of things, then you create the concept and it becomes human, the impression becomes human; but from a concept, it becomes again an image, that is, it becomes

poetry. It becomes the reconstructive reason, reconstructive, which converts the world.

*Péguy, in the piece that you suggested to us, describes hope as
a child in the middle of faith and charity, which are like two
adult women who are sort of raised by him, as if without hope,
they would remain stunted. But you were saying also that
without faith, hope can't exist. I want to understand what link
there is between these two things.*
Who knows the answer? What is the phenomenon that
makes man move; that "moves" him and therefore makes
him move?

*A persuasive encounter.*
*Desire.*
There, the persuasive encounter is a place, it indicates a
place. The desire for happiness is the answer.

But I had to realize, unfortunately through various experiences, that even a dog, when mealtime arrives, moves.
"What a restless dog you have." "It's time to feed him."
Before, he had been there lying down all day, motionless,
but come nine p.m. – his eating time – he moves, he walks
around, sniffs, poses a threat to the ham that's on the table;
even a dog moves for a desire, that in this case, is the
satisfaction of eating the ham.

Why does man have the desire for happiness? What
does man do to have the desire for happiness? The dog,
for example, doesn't have it – it moves because it has the
desire for something, but not for happiness. You can't
apply the word happiness to a dog, except by reducing it

to the word satisfaction. Man desires, moves out of a desire for happiness, because his nature is a thirst for total satisfaction, for truth, for happiness, for justice. What are these called in *The Religious Sense*? The needs of the heart, or in short, heart, as the Bible more rightly says. Because the word reason can be a kite that slips out of your hand and becomes pieces of paper that fly away in the sky, but the heart can't slip out of your hand and sail in the sky; papers are dry things, an expectation of arid things. While it's in the hands of a child, a kite is restrained by the child, so it's not pieces of paper; but if it becomes detached from the hands of the child, it becomes pieces of paper. The heart, no – the heart isn't a piece of paper. Therefore, the biblical word "heart" is more solid, more complete than the word we use, "reason."

But let's go back: the dog moves because it has a desire for food. Man moves because his nature is made for happiness, for fulfillment, for the satisfaction of his ultimate needs. What is the problem in the middle? For a dog, it's enough to follow his instincts; for man, you can't speak of instinct, you need to speak of awareness or knowledge. Man has the consciousness that he is made "for something." This is so true that a boy is right to ask himself, after having flunked five times: "What sense does life have?" (even if he would be more correct in asking himself why he flunked the fifth time!).

However, what is there in the midst of everything? A consciousness. This is so true that we can say: "I have the right to be satisfied. I have the right to not be destroyed; I have the right to be, to reach my destiny, I have the right to be treated with justice." This right is man's nature, man is self-aware, is conscious of himself. What does it mean that I am conscious of myself? That I know the principal things that make up my nature. My nature is such that it understands that it has the right to be able to reach the end of its road (otherwise, why travel the road?).

So the answer to the question – what is it? That faith makes you meet a factor that is present in the life of your "I," in your life, which is stronger again than nature. By nature, you say: "I have the right to justice: who knows?"; the term of natural sureness is the phrase "Who knows?" (who knows if ever, who knows what will be, what will be will be). But instead, faith is consciousness of a Presence in you and with you, more powerful than your nature, so much so that it doesn't allow you to say "Who knows?" If you would say "Who knows?" you'd offend that Presence. And it is a Presence that has the power to make you sure of reaching what you want, sure of what you are made for; it tells you what you are made for: "You are made for me." Just as Saint Augustine understood and repeated with that famous sentence: "The heart of man is made for God and is restless until it rests in Him."[43] It is made for Christ: "You are made for me." "I am the Way, the Truth and the Life,"[44] "Without me you can do nothing."[45] You cannot even pinpoint with certainty what you were born for. And here, faith begins.

Faith is the consciousness of a Presence that clarifies for you the aim of life, without the possibility of uncertainty – "I am the Truth and the Life." It is stronger and has such strength – "I love You, God, my strength." How can you, after having said an antiphon like this, not repeat it always? It has such strength that, with Him, you will attain what you are made for; with Him, you will reach Him. With Him, who journeys together with you, you will reach Him, the Word by which all the world comes into being. With Him, who journeys together with you, you watch Him and He's a man with a staff, like you, a man who is seated there at home and is speaking to you, and John, and Andrew ... (I, in front of God, at least one sin I will not have committed; I have always called you back to the two passages from the Gospel in front of which any Goliath collapses: the first chapter of Saint John, the second part, and the last chapter of Saint John, the last part).

He who journeys together with you – He who is there speaking at home with you, He who is there around the cooked fish at the dawn of that morning – He who journeys together with you tells you with certainty what you are made for. And you know what He tells you? "It is I, but not I as you see me here, I who in this moment am giving life to the universe," and therefore with His help, we'll reach Him, surprising Him while He is giving birth to all the flowers of the world and raising up all the mountains of the world and laying out the lakes, all the lakes of the world, and distributing the stars, all the stars of the sky. The only thing that I can't understand, because I've never understood it, is how you can possibly resist these things when they are so evidently definitive; it's not possible for man to find anything more beautiful!

Last night, I went with a friend to the home of friends (they were a lot of women; there must have been thirty-five – no, forty) and on leaving, he told me: "They have the responsibility of bringing to the world the reason that makes it worthwhile having children." Those people are people called to cry out to the world the *why*: the why of working, of living and of dying, of putting up with your wife, as happens in ninety-nine percent of the cases after one-and-a-half months of marriage.

If man is that level of nature in which nature becomes aware of itself, becoming aware of itself, the reflection introduces us to the fated garden of being. Faith makes the destiny you were made for certain, and it allows you to know it, it allows you to begin to know it; then, you move, then it is hope that draws out faith (as you wanted to show!). Hope is like a fire that draws out faith, draws out knowledge. Faith can be a struggle; hope makes it less of a struggle, it draws out faith.

This is so true that, with hope, you can more easily make a mistake, demand, make a claim, establish in advance when something has to happen. Did you understand in what sense Péguy spoke of hope that draws out faith (even if hope is based on faith)?

Faith founds, makes known, what man is made for, and therefore reveals to man what he desires; then man starts to move because he desires, and this is hope. Faith feels drawn bumpily along by hope. But the seriousness, the degree of seriousness, isn't given by hope, but by faith. The degree of seriousness is given by the truth, while the degree of zest and fascination is given by hope.

As we don't yet know well, we can't know our destiny, we can't know Christ as He is, except for as much as is revealed to us. In that way, faith, calmly, establishes the journey; and hope is all the indomitable thrill of children when a father says: "Let's go to see the train." I remember when I went to the beach with my father for the first time – I was nine. After via Pergolesi, at the light, there I was, tapping my feet because I wanted to see the train that was high above. Hope is like a child who stamps his feet, quivering. Slowly, as one grows up, quivering enlivens even curiosity regarding faith.

*Hope is based on a Presence and this Presence was described as possession. Later, you told us that you need to live life within an awareness of the relationship with Him. I would like to understand this better.*
The word "this" is a little indistinct. What did you want to understand? Repeat the words slowly so that we can understand. To understand Dante, you need to read him more than once; if, reading him one time through quickly, you claim to understand him, you don't understand anything (that's the way students prepare for exams!).

*Hope is based on, is founded on the Presence …*
Of all the sentences you could invent, think of or hear, this one is the greatest of all: hope, meaning the certainty of destiny, is tied to a Presence, something present. Watch out, because, per se, it would be a contradiction: awaiting something that will come is tied to the present! A child's arrival at the top of a mountain is tied to a Presence: that of his father who acts as guide. Go on with your question.

*Hope relies on a Presence, is based on a Presence.*

It's based on a Presence that you possess, a Presence that belongs to you (if you possess it, it belongs to you). But a Presence that belongs to you, a Presence that is your possession is also a Presence to which you belong.

A child belongs to his mother, you can also say that the child possesses his mother; his mother belongs to him and he belongs to her. Where one belongs to another, the inverse is always true: the other belongs to him, otherwise it's a terrible lie. So?

*I wanted to understand this better in the relationship between Jesus and myself.*

I've already told you almost everything. Hope needs something else present that it possesses and by which, thus, it is possessed. It's something that reveals to you what you're made for, and it gives you the strength to get there. This Presence is Jesus.

But think for a moment: until now, what has your life been in the face of this discovery? It's been nothing! In the face of the discovery that there's a Presence that belongs to you and that you possess, you possess Christ and He possesses you! With this Presence, you realize what your destiny is, where your destiny is, you're sure to make it there, and you walk there. Destiny is reached through a Presence, something present; of the present. Therefore, it has to do with the pen that you write with, it has to do with the nose that you look at, it has to do with your sleepiness, *it has to do with it, it has to do with it.* It has to do with anything that you look at or touch.

If Christ has nothing to do with what you touch and look at, it's not true that you are touching, it's not true that you are looking. It's not true that He has nothing to do with these things; rather, what's true is that you're not looking, touching, loving – your humanity isn't true. In fact, you're confused about your destiny and you're completely skeptical about the possibility of reaching your destiny. What is human is missing: in our doubt, it's not Christ that is missing, but rather our humanity. That's why Jesus said: "Thank you, Father, because you have revealed these things to the simple."[46] And, to the novices of subsequent years, as the first moral virtue of the person who follows Christ, we have cited simplicity, or better, sincerity, because sincerity is simplicity that passes through freedom. Simplicity can be a character trait, sincerity is a virtue.

If you don't understand something, speak up. At least have compassion for the way that I'm explaining.

*You said that these words are clear and abstract and this, in itself, is apparently a contradiction.*
It's not a contradiction. Clear and abstract can go very well together. Hegel is clear and abstract; but maybe you don't know who Hegel is!

*I wanted to ask you to explain it to me because I understand that the words appear clear, but then it's as if what remains isn't a distance but …*
If you hear a word that is clear, that word blows away in the wind, it goes away with the wind if you don't look at it, don't fix your gaze on it, that is, if you're not interested

in it. For it to feel abstract, it has to be uninteresting to you. First, it has to be uninteresting to you, then it will feel abstract.

Therefore, when you hear these things and they seem abstract, first, you shouldn't be surprised, because it's part of the temptation that original sin perennially left in us; it's part of the demon, of the devil, of the lie, of the lie that rests fundamentally in us. In us, there's a contradiction, in us there's a complication for which obvious things – obvious means that they lie in front of us in the path – seem complicated, seem difficult.

Aside from this, which is a premise for you, for me, for everyone, the norm of our behaviour, actually, lies in this: either something is clear, or it's not clear to you, or you invent pretexts to say it's not clear when it should be clear to you. In the second case, you need to unravel the tangle, but in the third case, there's no remedy: if it's clear, it feels abstract to you only if you're not interested in it; you decide it's not interesting to you and so it feels abstract.

Like a person, a beautiful silhouette that passes along the other side of the street and you catch a glimpse of it as you're quickly walking by, worrying about your affairs; you see it, you take note of it (maybe the day after you say: "I saw a beautiful silhouette yesterday in the street"), but you don't stop to look at it, you don't even remember the colour of the dress or the hair, because you weren't interested, you were interested in other things.

This is profoundly true with respect to our destiny, our relationship with Christ Jesus, with God and with Christ. But it's also profoundly true with respect to our relationship with our father, mother, siblings, and friends. The more one is close to you, your friend, the more you don't understand the clearest things in him or her; they are abstract because you don't permit them to have anything to do with you. If a person is very close to you, and you don't allow something clear that you see in him to have anything to do with you, that clear thing slides by quickly, and you're left without anything; at most, you can speak about it in the opposite sense, you tell lies about it, because it didn't interest you. For example, if you have a brother who plays soccer and you don't care one whit about soccer, you're crazy for basketball, then when your brother talks about soccer, (because Juventus lost, lost against Inter, and you go to school or to work and you hear that even your classmates are tearing their hair out because of Inter, Juventus ...) you don't care in the least bit, you're perfectly indifferent. Meanwhile, at the announcement that Philadelphia's basketball team lost to Boston, you light up right away, you go all over the place, you check all the newspapers to be sure about the news. Are you with me?

Let's summarize: something clear becomes abstract, that is, fleeting – the abstract is what is fleeting – if first you've discarded your interest, if you're not interested in life felt and lived, if you have decided to be interested in other things.

What do you have to do in this case? In this case you must fix your gaze. While the word, seeming abstract to you, tends to slide by, you need to fix your gaze on it – you need to look back to where the silhouette is going and fix your gaze on it – fix your gaze on that word, repeat that word to yourself and say: "Explain this word." You need to fix your gaze on that word in every way possible: "What does it have to do with the interests that I live, *now*?" Then, it may be that, at a certain point, you feel heat flowing inside you, and you begin to understand it, to feel it.

*The last time you spoke of dream and of ideal hope.*
*I'm discovering I have the temptation to live immediate hope as*
*a dream and to postpone ideal hope. I want to understand*
*this better.*

Well, how have we defined ideal hope? How have we defined the ideal? The ideal identifies the need for which the heart is made, therefore it comes at the end, its fulfill-ment is in the future; you're on a path. What ideal hope is, then, is clear. But that reflects either a little or a lot on the form and the feeling of the circumstances you're living in *now*.

That you made the present a dream is a mask for the temptation to not commit yourself in the present. Now, if you're in a good mood, you build a dream, you build the image of what you should do in the present, and you only do what you yourself stress.

Wait while I give you a comparison: to make a comparison means to live! So, mathematics homework – at least it used to happen to me this way (you see "it used to happen to me this way:" it's a memory, a thing I lived; if I hadn't lived it I wouldn't be able to make the comparison!) – mathematics homework: if I don't feel like doing it I say:

"Yes, yes, all right, all right," and I turn it in. The teacher right away says: "Look at what a mistake you made on the first line!" I treated the mathematical problem as if it were a dream. Since I didn't feel like it ...

Therefore the true response to your question is within the answer to that previous one our friend asked. Man discovers, therefore knows, and creates what he loves; where, then, you understand that love is not a dream, only to the degree that it is the correct anticipation of final happiness. For this reason the words "I love you" are a lie ninety-nine percent of the time; they have to be restrained and guided, well-measured, well-proportioned, if they're going to be correct, so they become powerful, so they become like hope, so they are no longer a child who draws faith and charity, but a horse that draws two carriages full of every grace of God, a zealous horse!

In the face of an object, you have a repulsion or an attraction (repulsion and indifference are the same, in the same way hate and strangeness are the same: strangeness is the beginning of hate; indifference is the beginning of repulsion). This is your dream, that is, reality as you bend it, in the form in which you bend it, that interests you, instead of making you become interested in reality as it is. "Reality as it is" is being in the desert and suddenly seeing the path, the path to the ideal. What was our problem?

*You then said: Christian life makes you live the present with such attention that it makes you see the little point that is destiny about to arrive, and it's a great day when you become aware of*

*this. I would like to know what it means to say that it is destiny*
*that is about to arrive.*

A boy, a young guy – he's twenty-four years old – is very much in love with a girl who is seventeen years old; he met her at the supermarket! The girl came from the Canary Islands; he takes her to the bridge where the little boats leave for the Canary Islands, for Tenerife (we are, evidently, on a pier in Seville!). The boat is full and begins to move off and go away. He follows all the movements of the boat with melancholy, and the farther away the boat gets the smaller it becomes. Translated into terms that aren't supposed but real, the farther away the boat gets, the farther away the girl gets, the more she slips from his hands, the more she becomes impossible to grasp. Until all that's left is the image, the image that he can carry wherever, but it's an image that wears out with time.

A guy was enrolled in Catholic Action, but later he encountered a movement called Communion and Liberation, and he met Guido: he went to college, and through his friendship with Guido he decided to begin the *verifica*.[47] But his destiny was other. He did the *verifica* seriously, but he saw in retrospect with the months that passed that it was a dream and not something real; with his great vexation, with his humiliation, he understood that he was made for the normal life (to be made for the normal life is never a beautiful intuition, never, and this is so true that something that I'm about to say happens to make it a dignified thing). That's to say that he falls in love with a girl. Now, Don Giorgio says: "No, no, look, don't listen to Guido anymore, listen more to Alberto." He's twenty-three years old, is finishing college, she is twenty-two, and in her last year. Since both of them are in CL, they have a seriousness and an interest nourished by the School of Community – because the School of Community is the greatest grace you can receive, and may God punish you if you don't use it well. No, may He not punish you, or else ... since you don't use it well! So they grow, they grow well. One works in the parish and the other works in the CL office, they give all the time possible and imaginable, they hardly ever see each other (which is the best sign for an affective relationship: he who doesn't live this sign doesn't truly love). At a certain point, to sum up, she has to go to Trieste, because she's graduating in languages from Trieste, and has to be away for six months. Since they aren't rich she can't say: "In a month I'll come home." It is right after Easter and Christmas is far off. With neither Easter nor Christmas to observe, she can't come home. Six months! So he is like the one who is seated on the bridge in Seville waiting for the ship to arrive. He anticipates, he waits, and the ship has yet to arrive. At a certain point – after three and three-quarter months! – on the horizon he sees a little point: she's ahead of schedule! That small point that approaches little by little becomes larger, becomes large, becomes large, you can see that it is indeed a small ship. At the bow of the ship a little, little girl is waving a handkerchief: it is she! It's the opposite of before. If their relationship is good, is right, she for him is the sign God has given, temporarily, to carry out his task in life. If he looks at her with these eyes, that girl is like the destiny that has drawn near to him and said: "I will accompany you for the length of the road until we return together."

First the ship goes far away, it becomes a little point and vanishes. In the second case, when man looks at things with truth, when he looks at things with clarity, when he looks at things within the ideal, then all things become a sign of his destiny. Just as the small flower of the field didn't escape Jesus, the child playing didn't escape Jesus, the poor woman at the well didn't escape Him, the most hated one in all of Jericho, who was perched in the tree to see Him, didn't escape Him; nothing escaped Him.

Everything becomes a sign of our destiny if we look at things seeing the relationship with Jesus, living the relationship with the Presence. If destiny is Presence, by living the relationship with this Presence, all things become a sign of it. A sign of it, just as the little point on the horizon is a sign of destiny that is about to arrive. If we live the relationship with the presence of Jesus, all things become signs.

How you manage to treat things without them becoming signs, this you yourselves will explain to me! Because I understand that one can be incoherent, and incoherence is a sharp if not agonizing pain, but the fact that you can look at things without awareness of the Presence of which they are a sign is something that at a certain point is not understandable – is not understandable! – because you no longer remember when you were young. Only children can look at things not as a sign. If you live the relationship with the Lord, anything is a sign. The more something interests you, the more it is a sign. Sign of what? Sign of the destiny that is about to arrive; but that destiny that is about to arrive is already there ... a sign of the One who is already there. This is so true that to treat your father or mother or wife or daughter well is to treat Him well, isn't it? Destiny is Presence, it's the same thing: What does God incarnate mean? Destiny made Presence.

Therefore everything is Presence and according to that which God has destined you, you see it as a small point hardly hinted at on the horizon or you see it as a closer speck or you see it as something with which you work today, nearby, in the same ambit.

In any case, one who has the vocation to virginity is called to live these things daily, always, and to remain so responsible as to be able to explain why sustaining the burden of having children is reasonable. The vocation to virginity is the ideal function for what all the others do, if they do it correctly. So, no one can love a person as one called to virginity and, in fact, one of the things I have to complain about with Gruppo Adulto is the necessity for them to use reason more, to love reason and have more affection, live affection more. No one is called to use reason and to live affection more than we are. That in which others usually seem to surpass us is only something extremely precise and limited, that which all beings, even inferior beings, have in common: instinct. The more one lives this inquiry – who knows, I would like to know the etymology of the word *indagine* [inquiry]: *in ago*, to act within, perhaps? To act within things, penetrate things – from the presence of Christ, to the presence of Truth and of infinite Love – to know and to love things and persons. The more one lives this inquiry, the more he or she feels for others, small, poor ... the truth is that they are all lost. For this reason it is worth the pain of any sacrifice, so that our inquiry may be deeper, our possession of the One who is present may be greater, and so, through this, others may understand more.

*What does hope have to do with the experience we're having now, with the beginning of vocation?*
Is there anyone who wants to answer this?

*"The One who began a good work in you will go on completing it until the Day of Jesus Christ comes."*[48]
He repeated Saint Paul's sentence. "He will go on completing it" is the definition of hope: certainty; certainty for the future is hope. "He who began in you this good work," because vocation comes to you from Another.

The word vocation is the reverberation of a Presence, the step of a Presence, of the Presence of destiny, which is companionship to you and dictated by the One for whom you are made; certainty of destiny and love for destiny. Vocation is that to which this voice calls. By its nature then, being called to a vocation like this makes hope gigantic, but, before making it gigantic, it claims hope, it requires hope. Without hope vocation dies.

Saint Paul's sentence, recited by Mandy, however, remains a fulfilled response. "The One who began this good work in you [what is good work? Vocation, we said before: there is no greater work than vocation, which is the recalling of the entire universe and all of history, the witness to the entire universe and to all of history that the road is

Christ and destiny is Christ, that destiny accompanies you on the road to yourself], will bring it to fulfillment" [and this is hope, it's the definition of hope, because hope is a certainty].

In my opinion, the gravest problem is the one indicated by our friend: that the word is clear and is abstract, and the remedy for this is to look it in the face, to continually look at it. Look at it also means to ask Mario: "Mario, explain this thing to me. Re-explain this thing. What does this thing mean for you? Why is this thing concrete? For example, now, why is it concrete?" The more you fix your gaze on this thing, the more you ask these questions, the more clarity will begin to coincide with the consistency of something present and with the suggestiveness of something felt.

*What does it mean that weariness and pain are enemies of hope? Why did you say: "The enemies of this faithfulness to belonging are discontinuity, weariness, and pain?"*
Enemies means the type of event that tries to impede faithfulness to hope. And they are: first, discontinuity. Discontinuity is one time in the dust, one time on the altar; like a cyclothymic, one time he laughs and two minutes after he cries. It is the non-linearity in maintaining the right frame of mind.

Second, weariness, and you know what weariness is. Weariness is an enemy, it is a temptation against faithfulness.

Third, the pain that is the sharpest aspect of weariness; even pain is an enemy, in the sense that pain tends to make us be unfaithful; one curses in front of pain. Like the mother of the adolescent they were bringing to the cemetery, who Jesus met in those fields just outside the town of Nain, while she shouted in her pain. For her the pain in that moment was the opposite of hope, so much so that Jesus tells her: "Woman, don't cry," trying to instill it in her like that, like a shock, at least a surprise. She would be surprised: a stranger passing by touches her shoulder, telling her: "Woman, don't cry." How is one able to tell a mother who is following the funeral procession of her son, her only son, "Don't cry," beginning, like that, to bring her back to taking herself into consideration? After that remark, even she will feel estranged; she will have suspended her shouts for a minute and in that instant Jesus resuscitates her son.

Therefore, discontinuity, weariness, pain. Discontinuity is an error, it's a weakness of character. Weariness is to put character to the test: even if very strong, it tests it, it puts it to the test. And pain then conquers everything; pain, if it doesn't have any hope of a response, conquers everything; some strong Hercules, in front of pain without an answer, gives in.

*In the fourth point you said that the most acute aspect of the struggle to keep belonging is forgiveness, that is the asking to be forgiven. Could you explain it better for me?*
Well, if rebellion towards faithfulness to the Mystery that made us, and that makes us complete this difficult journey, has as its opposite discontinuity, trial, pain, why are these things in opposition? Because they aren't according to what

you want. Discontinuity, trial, pain are against trust in God, because God doesn't do what you want, things don't happen the way you expected them to. It is original sin activating itself historically according to its consequences, which means it is man's claim of possessing his own life but, instead, life happens in a different way.

Now, the claim of our possessing our life, where does it touch the depths of humiliation? The depths of humiliation for me who tries to possess my life in my own hands, is that my life, in order to be, to continue, needs Another to forgive it. Forgiveness is the most difficult thing to accept because it is precisely a ripping away of our presumption at its roots. To be forgiven means to feel the claim we have of possessing ourselves and of fulfilling our own lives torn out by the roots. We are not capable, and therefore we always mess up. We aren't capable, we rebel, and then all the things we do – I said this before – all the things we do don't hold up, aren't right: relationships with people, with things, with ourselves aren't ever right and we don't succeed in straightening everything out.

Nevertheless there's a strength in us, the strength that creates us, that embraces us just the same, while we grow agitated like naughty children, it embraces us just the same. It's from this embrace that our agitation subsides and we recognize Him to whom we belong. We don't want to belong if not to ourselves and so we mess everything up, but He to whom we belong embraces us just the same. Now, at this point, one gives in. Like a child who plays around and the mother, instead of spanking him, hugs him:

he squirms around a little in her arms, but after a little he cries. Do you understand?

Forgiveness leaves the strongest temptation of humiliation that man has because the strongest temptation man has is that of being master of himself. Needing to be forgiven is its most terrible opposite. Therefore to accept forgiveness is really man's greatest struggle. If they hadn't been forgiven, the people of Israel would have been stuck at the second or third stage, because in two stages they had already rebelled three times. To be forgiven is the greatest struggle we have to weather, because being forgiven means understanding that you truly belong to Another and it's this Other who makes us what we ought to be; who, touching us, gives us the strength to resume the path.

*You said that hope is the second constitutive factor of the Christian personality. Why did you say this? And what stake does freedom have in hope?*
You will help me understand the why of your question! First of all, hope is a factor of the personality. What is the first factor of the personality?

*Faith.*
For a Bantu it is faith?

*It is reason.*
The first virtue of the personality, the first factor of the personality is faith, for which man's situation was illuminated. The Bantu deludes himself, thinking his own strength

suffices to construct the first factor. Reason doesn't hold up, all the energy of his strength doesn't hold up, isn't enough, not even to complete one correct gesture, said Ibsen in *Brand*.[49] Faith is the first factor because it's the factor that makes you know the condition for being able to exist, for being able to be on your feet and walking, which is the presence of Another.

Hope is the second constitutive factor of the personality because the personality is constituted *hic et nunc*, now, but to walk towards something of Another, that is in the future, that isn't here yet. Even clarity and strength to walk towards the future is given by Another. Thus hope is the continuity, it is the consequence of faith towards the future.

And so what are you asking me?

*Where does my freedom come into play?*
Thus I understand that I can't stand up by myself, the help of Another is necessary. For example, to get out of a car, if my knees hurt from arthritis, it's difficult for me to stand up, so someone comes over to help me. And I, in front of the image of a little old man that one helps out of the car and gets on his feet, I rebel: one comes to help me, I don't want it. Hope is the capacity to confront the future with clarity and strength, overcoming the temptations of pain, weariness, discontinuity, or trials with the help of Another, of the presence of Another, which is the continuity of faith. Freedom either accepts this Other or doesn't accept it; it can accept it or not accept it; it can accept the hand that comes to help or it can reject it.

Freedom is produced immediately as acceptance or rejection, as yes or as no; and the most elementary and decisive form of acceptance is called asking. In asking one participates in the gesture that helps him, therefore in asking full freedom begins. If one comes to help me and pull me out of the car, I can say no, I can try to get out by myself; I can unwillingly accept the hand that sustains me; but I can desire the hand that sustains me, accept asking for it: and here, it is in the asking that my freedom is established in its fullness.

*You reminded us that the most urgent problem for us is that these things risk remaining clear, but abstract, and you told us to fix our gaze on these words, asking and following, indicating for us a relationship as the way of getting out of this discomfort. Help for coming out of this abstraction, for us in the first year,[50] is to live a relationship.*

For you of the first year or for me of the fiftieth, of the eightieth year! What does it mean to exist? To live a relationship: if you don't live a relationship with being, you don't exist. Thus what you say now is nothing more than the prolongation of your origin, it's the same phenomenon. To live a relationship, accept a relationship. The most complete expression, where the expression becomes fulfilled, where acceptance of the relationship flowers fully, is called asking.

Therefore, in the face of these problems that seem clear but abstract, I've replied first to our friend that they seemed abstract to him even though they were clear, because he had first rejected them; they didn't interest him before. And in fact there is a category that he rejected: "clear but abstract" isn't to say "correct but abstract." "Clear" means that I speak in logical terms, "correct" means that it is pertinent to life, that it helps life, that it sustains life. This thing is correct for my life, even if it seems abstract. Now you understand what Anna was saying before.

*I said that the path you indicated to us wasn't that of addressing ourselves to a personal analysis: I who set out to immerse myself in these new things that Gruppo Adulto teaches me ...*

... that is, I put myself in front of the words, of the sentences, of the logical links that the discussion by Gruppo Adulto proposes to me. This is analysis, everything remains abstract: clear, very clear. "I have no objections," but it is abstract. Instead it is "correct," it isn't just clear. We need to reach the concept of correct, which means that my life without destiny is the life of a dog and it's a life that's going to end in corruption. Correct, we need something correct! Even if it's abstract, it's necessary for me; I recognize that it's necessary for me, although it is abstract; I still don't understand, I still don't hear, I still don't see: this is human.

To make the "correct" concrete and not abstract I must make the effort to establish relationships, to live relationships. For example, why are we obligated to be in a companionship? It's an application of the necessity of these relationships. Because the Didache, one of the first Christian writings, says: "Every day look for the faces of the saints and take comfort in their discussions."[51] It's a relationship.

In a relationship, slowly, the correct — which you still don't understand, so it seems abstract — begins to become concrete. You learn love as gratuitousness and as tenderness from a person who lives love as gratuitousness and tenderness, you don't learn it theoretically. You learn life in the concrete, not theoretically. Remember this last thing that was said. It is in relationships that Being develops. The form that the metallic incandescence of Being assumes is relationships.

*Working on what you told us about hope …*
Excuse me, let's not use the word work often because it has overtones of labour union activity; instead let's use the word meditate or reflect, which is a little more human, less the fruit of pure organization.

*Being with people where I live, it seems exactly that for the world, hope is to wait for something to happen tomorrow that is different from today. Instead, for me, slowly, slowly, by grace, it is exactly an asking that what happened to me embrace me again tomorrow, and that I can embrace it again like today, even more, in the concrete faces of this companionship. And when it happens this way I realize that it is a construction where I am, in the sense that a positive outlook on reality happens. I wanted to ask if this was correct.*
It isn't only correct, but I invite everyone to fix his gaze on this statement because of the depth of its suggestion. That which characterizes hope let's say "of the world," instinctive and natural hope, is that tomorrow be different

from today, different in that which today was difficult, unfulfilled. And instead she says: no, hope is that tomorrow I may have the capacity, the strength, to embrace what happens, what "re-happens," because normally "the more" of what will happen tomorrow is something that happens today also, that happened yesterday. That I have the strength to accept what will happen or will re-happen tomorrow, in such a way that – you said it – I can embrace it and make it constructive.

In this way it becomes evident that the world's hope is fragmentary and makes life fragmentary: one piece and another piece different from the first. It makes life fragmented. While Christian hope, from what happens or re-happens or changes in the happening, draws forth a new image from everything; that is, it constructs, it makes the construction grow.

*With regard to what you said about the Pygmies who prayed to God, I wanted to know why and if it's true that God didn't respond to them.*

He didn't respond, in fact He had no intention of responding. But not the Pygmies. The pygmies named Bobbio, the pygmies named Kafka, the pygmies named Camus, the pygmies who are the greatest expressers of the human, the pygmies named Wagner, the pygmies named Homer or Virgil, the pygmies who are named the great thinkers. No one was given a reply, no one replied. We have to be careful not to superimpose the fixed image we were given by grace on a situation that by its nature remains uncertain, obscure, and tangled.

In fact, to make Himself known, God had to respond to that question; God had to take a step Himself and say: "Here I am." "Phillip, who sees me, sees the Father."[52] It was the only case in history and it's precisely this case that is unbearable to everyone. Those three hundred heads of religion who made the symbolic procession from San Carlo to the Duomo all agreed that no one could claim to exactly know the solution. There were three hundred attempts and not one of the three hundred said: "We have the answer." No one witnessed it – prudently – otherwise three hundred God-seekers couldn't have gotten together. They were all seekers of God. We are seekers of a God whose name and whose face are well-known: we know the name and the face.

*So then it's useless for one who doesn't know Christ to ask?*
No! Christ is the answer to all of humanity's questions. When Leopardi said: "If thou among the eternal/ ideas art numbered, which the eternal mind /deigns not should e'er be clothed in fleshly form/ And in frail human frames/ learn what ills our mortal life doth swarm;/ Or if some other earth be thine of those/ Innumerable worlds wherewith heav'n flames/ And, brighter than the Sun, the nearest star/ Through kinder atmosphere above thee glows;/ From here, where days are brief and skies soon darken,/ To this, an unknown lover's hymn, oh hearken,"[53] he was asking Beauty to make herself visible and to make him love her. It was a question, the question about something that had already happened one thousand eight-hundred years before him, and he didn't know it.

*So He responds in a different way?*
No, God responds in a precise way: it's called Christ. A man born of a woman in that hovel – when you go to Palestine it's the most moving moment of the entire pilgrimage – where it's written in bronze: *Verbum caro hic factum est*, the Word was made flesh here. It's an answer. We can only know God if He reveals Himself.

Analogously, this is true for us. A person doesn't become known if he doesn't reveal himself, say who he is. A great psychologist or a great "knower" of men and women, a great penetrator of consciences can understand many things to the degree that, without realizing it, the other reveals himself; but the other has to reveal himself, if he isn't revealed he doesn't understand. The spirit is mysterious with regard to that investigation of the precise reality made through the eyes, the senses, and reason. Do you understand me, Silvia? Tell me what isn't convincing you.

*And so, the Pygmies who do not know Christ?*
The Pygmies who do not know Christ asked to know God in their own way. And, not even that: they asked God to help them; because a baby's way of knowing is that of being helped.

*And he replied?*
He replied according to his own plan. The major portion of the faces seemed not to reply; at times they seemed to reply. But always "seemed," because it wasn't according to the form of their minds that he replied.

In fact, they asked; instead of having hurried, they waited, they had to wait and wait and wait, until a strange, white person with a beard came (maybe he was a Verona Father or perhaps a missionary from the White Fathers); he went to them and said: "The God who went out to hunt has come back and is here among us."

God always replies. But God's reply cannot coincide with the dynamic of our thinking, unless it is taken unawares in its origins: now it's a correct dynamic, you understand the reply. In fact it's a dynamic without end. The need for happiness, for justice, for love – what images do these have? They are angles that are open to the infinite, they don't have a conclusive form insofar as all loves, all truths, all justices aren't enough. Having arrived there, at the crest of the hill – Thomas Mann would say in *Joseph and His Brothers*[54] – having arrived at the crest of the hill he saw another crest, having arrived at that crest he saw another, right up to the infinite, indefinitely. He described the banks of the North Sea and the dunes that stopped in the sea. It's a nice comparison; life translates this comparison into action.

It's for this that Von Speyr wrote that famous sentence, that God always makes things happen in a way that generates an oversight:[55] You ask for health, He gives you glanders (in a manner of speaking) and then you say: "God was bad to me." No, why did you ask for health? You asked for health to give glory to God, that is to reach the dignity of your person in such a way that would be commensurable with the Eternal, with the Infinite. So, to have this, God understands that he has to give you glanders, he makes you bear the weight of a grave illness.

It's what you have understood well, and witnessed in the most beautiful way yet, with Clemente Rebora in his poetry, in his conversion and his poetry. The poetry of Clemente Rebora is something you should read because, contrary to what we're used to (what we're used to is that when someone converts it's as if his poetic vein becomes arid, and it's understandable: when one converts he understands an object that's much more interesting than the objects that interested him before and therefore even poetry becomes dung for him, to use the words of Saint Paul) Rebora's poetic vein had such a new impetus, that Eugenio Montale would always go visit him, especially when he was ill, in Stresa.

*Is the moral attitude a grace or the fruit of an education?*
The moral attitude is above all the fruit of an act that creates you, therefore it's essentially a grace. Originally it's a grace because the moral attitude is the position in which the gesture of God that gives you life creates you. This is so true that in *Un avvenimento di vita cioè una storia*[56] it says that the moral law is to maintain oneself in the original position in which the creative act made us, which is therefore that of being children: a child, not exalted or already adulterated by extraneous influences, a child in curiosity and openness, curiosity and adhesion.

I haven't finished answering, because if you stop me here, where is freedom? She said: "Is the moral attitude the fruit of an education or a grace?." If the education of a child doesn't insist on the original attitudes in which he was created, for example on sincerity, on dependence, on wonder, on fineness, on delicacy, on the measure in relationships ... if these original characteristics aren't underlined, time evaporates them, takes away their light. Therefore they're like brooks that lose their banks: they overflow and the water that seeps over ultimately damages, unless it spread within stabilized confines, with order; the water that overflows becomes a swamp or destroys.

And so everyone grows up without an education and loses his original perceptions; they have the gall to say: "But for me this isn't virtue, I don't feel it." Especially certain virtues, dangerous from the point of view of the commitment they exact: "I don't feel those things: I don't feel it's bad to disobey, I don't feel that impurity is bad, I don't feel it's bad to ..." How is it "I don't feel, I don't feel?" They go against what they originally perceived.

Why does the Church demand that babies, to be baptized, have a community around them represented by the godparents? The godparents aren't like the two candles, fulfilling the form, even a dramatic one, in the dialogue with the priest; the godparents aren't worth anything if they aren't representatives of the community. Therefore when I celebrate a baptism I always say the godparents are there as representatives of the community.

So then, morality is remaining in the position in which God originally created you, and this is grace; without the fulfillment of the context, without education those seeds do not develop. If the soil isn't good, the seed doesn't develop or develops very poorly, develops with extreme effort. What is given us as grace is given to man as freedom, and therefore man can accept it or not, can accept corresponding to it or not.

How many people – not even old people, adults – at a certain point in a discussion, when they don't know what else to say, express nostalgia for when they were small. Why nostalgia for when they were little? Nostalgia for the time in which you had to use freedom and you didn't use it, you used it poorly.

One who is on the path is obligated to have the courage and sincerity to say "I made a mistake"; to say "Lord, I made a mistake" burns the mistake, because it makes the truth quickly win out, makes the truth win out over the mistake.

*The fact that the good that we hope for is arduous, it costs something to have it, causes an objection. Why do we have this attitude, as if we shouldn't have to make an effort?*
We have this resentment towards the fact that for life to achieve the good we must make an effort – so that the heart's desired good is arduous to reach – exactly because the heart was given to us as a need for happiness. Being given to us as a need for happiness, we say: "We'll have to find it at a good price"; because it was a grace to have the need for happiness, being able to achieve it should at least be at a good price.

Instead God died on the cross to make everyone see that achieving it must exact a toll, must imply a sacrifice: this is the big word. But without sacrifice you can't put up with looking at the face of a person you love for one minute. You can't look at it a minute without sacrifice, without accepting a sacrifice.

Look: we and God, responding to the encounter we had with Jesus, that is with God made man, understand only that which we arrive at through human experience. Ratzinger says it,[57] with other words: only something that has passed through our experience becomes reasonable for us – that is, can be welcomed and approved by us. Therefore even the tribulation of temptation, the tests of affections, the effort to be pure, the effort of coherence, of justice, are all experiences through which man is conducted by God to be more like Christ, to be more fulfilled.

*But arduous isn't opposed to simple.*
Arduous isn't opposed to simple. Simple indicates the way in which you can confront arduousness. Without simplicity you don't confront arduousness because, if you look at arduousness without simplicity, you say: "But, if, but, maybe, perhaps," which are all words that are the most sordid and satanic enemies of the perception of truth. Even if you were in front of a beautiful face, if you don't love it, you find all the pretexts to say: "Here, but, but, it has a little pimple here, a little black pimple here, it has a yellow pimple there, it has a nose that's lightly misplaced to the left, lightly misplaced to the right, etcetera."

*Speaking of patience, you said that with respect to the weight of reality, we have two possible positions: either a more superficial*

*position, through which we forget the weight of today and say*
*"Let's enjoy it as long as we can"; or a more serious attitude,*
*that you defined as stoic magnanimity, in which we take this*
*weight upon ourselves. But you also said we are like Atlas,*
*who takes a step, and this weight crushes him.*
Perfect.


*And you said that patience is much closer to this second attitude.*
*Exactly because this magnanimity cannot be sustained by*
*ourselves, I wanted to ask you how close patience is to this and*
*where the distinction is.*
Patience is close to this to the degree that it has to suffer,
that is, put up with this; it's the concept of patience as for-
bearance; but this is distinct from stoic magnanimity to the
degree that it is its opposite, to the degree that it's a humble
certainty of the strength of Another.

"I have the strength for everything through Him who
empowers me,"[58] said Saint Paul. This sentence removes
whatever pretext we can have against the path and it
removes whatever pretext of desolation or of discourage-
ment in front of whatever error. Therefore it saves the path
and saves one from errors.

All of our effort is to bring ourselves to perceive the
original simplicity of the relationship between God and
man. When Christ looked at Magdalene with a furtive
glance on the street, it was a simple thing: it was a call to
her with simplicity and a simplicity in which purity domi-
nated and re-dominated; contrary to her history, but not
contrary to her present possibility.

Beer! How nice of you. So then it's a nice indication for the future: it's the second time and there are not two without three. Establish two points and you establish a straight line that goes to the infinite.

To the health of the one who thought of it and of everyone!

## 2 Poverty

### FROM HOPE, POVERTY

Today we have to see what is born from hope, which is none other than the expanding of the certainty of faith regarding the future. It is this that interests us: the present doesn't interest us as much as the future; for man, his origin doesn't interest him as much as his destiny. What can we derive from this expansion of the certainty regarding the future, that is called hope? Trust must be a dominant virtue, a characteristic virtue of this passage; the weapon with which man combats the uncertainty of the future is trust. Through hope, faith becomes trust.

But we're not going to linger on this today, I would like to look at the passage. As the passage from faith to obedience is freedom – because freedom allows obedience: the obstacle to obedience can come from freedom – so from hope to trust the obstacle that can be born is the attribution of the certainty in the future to particular things we already possess: for example, money, hair, gold eyeglasses, friendships, the protection of elders, knowing how to sing, muscles ... according to all versions and images.

What could hinder trust, in the same manner in which freedom can arouse and impede obedience? I've almost already said it just now: something we possess, in which we specifically place our trust; something we already possess. But then, it has to do with non-possession; at least in that way, it has to do with non- possession, and the virtue that has to do with non-possession is poverty.

As the virtue of freedom opens up the space for obedience, so the virtue of poverty opens up the space for trust ... which is paradoxical, because freedom and obedience seem contradictory, and the space that non-possession opens up for trust seems contradictory; no, it *is* contradictory. Instead, in Christian discourse, according to its usual unpredictability, according to its unexpected attitude, hope, above all, gives birth to poverty.

## 1   DO NOT HOPE FOR FUTURE HAPPINESS BASED ON A PARTICULAR PRESENT POSSESSION

We can begin to define poverty starting with the external. Starting with the external, like external spectators, we could define poverty in the terms suggested by hope; hope suggested to us the certainty of a good in the future, certainty in the future due to a certainty of the present: the certainty of Christ present opens up certainty for the future.

Poverty makes this possible precisely because it doesn't make us hope for future happiness from a *particular* present possession; the *particular* present possession would be contrary to faith. It makes us hope for the future, for future happiness, because of the presence of Christ, because of the possession of Christ present. Poverty saves this hope for the future, it doesn't obstruct this hope for the future, because it stops us from putting our hope in a *particular* present possession; not in the possession of Christ present, but in a *particular* present possession, or in the present possession of a *particular* thing. Poverty is not to place hope in a *particular* possession: *particular* means fixed by us, foreseen by us, chosen among what is comfortable to us, chosen among what persuades us more, chosen among what gives us more richness and therefore economic security. *Particular*: *quidam*, not *aliquis*, but *quidam*.

Non-poverty is opposed to hope because it places security in a future happiness on a *particular* possession, that can be present or future: "I hope to win seven million in the lottery tomorrow." With seven million I say to my soul: "My soul, eat and drink, rest assured because now you have everything," like the rich man in the gospel. "Fool!" Jesus tells him. "This very night the demand will be made for your soul; and this hoard of yours, *cujus erunt*? Whose will it be then?"[1] Therefore the opposition is that a *particular* possession − present or future, I don't care − makes me place my hope in it; this means that hope is no longer a response to Christ. Hope is the certainty in Christ that becomes the foundation of certainty for the future; certainty resting on something I fix upon, present or future, is opposed to hope. The girl has the guy;

everything's great! A few months or years pass with the certainty of having everything: this is a non-poor relationship. Not because one shouldn't have the guy in a serious way, but because the certainty of her hope, the certainty for her future, rests on that; and ninety-nine per cent of the time it happens that way ... point ninety-nine, I forgot!

I feel that I am impelled to make you understand this because it is the most important thing: I have certainty in the future, this certainty in the future comes from a present: I possess Christ. Faith makes me recognize Christ present, I possess Christ and thus I am certain for the future, this is hope. What opposes this hope is any manner in which man fixes his gaze on something that is determined by him, chosen by him, either in the present or in the future – it's all the same.

The whole mechanism lies in placing certainty in something, in a *particular* thing, in a *particular* possession on which then our hope depends. Our hope doesn't depend on Christ, it depends on a *particular* possession, on the possession of a *particular* thing, *cuiusdam rei*.

What is this premise saying? That there isn't anything on which you can place your hope; you can't place your hope for the future on any possession, because whatever you possess is taken away by tomorrow, by time or by a bicycle: the bicycle that violently hits the individual; he falls and, falling, knocks his head on the sidewalk and dies. The next day, instead of celebrating his wedding, you go to his funeral.

## From the certainty that "God fulfills," the freedom of things

Let's go deeper with the question, the first step is to go deeper. On what, then, does poverty found its value? On the certainty that it is God who fulfills; Christ fulfills the desire that He creates in you: "He who began this good work in you will bring it to fulfillment tomorrow in the day of Christ."[2] The foundation of poverty is in the certainty that God fulfills what He makes you desire.

If God, God present, Christ – because God works through Christ – if Christ gives you the certainty of fulfilling what He makes you desire, then you are extremely free from things. The image of freedom is born – most of all, freedom from things. You are a slave of nothing, you are bound to nothing, you are enchained to nothing, you depend on nothing: you are free. The word freedom is more correct, in front of *you're bound, you depend*. They are all verbs that can represent a lived occurrence, but the original characteristic aspiration of every lived occurrence is a freedom. Now, you are not a slave of what you use, because you are *only* a slave of Him who gives you the certainty of your happiness. Poverty is revealed as freedom from things inasmuch as it is God who fulfills desires, not the *particular* thing that you are admiring.

We are not saying abstract things, because for such and such a girl to have a certain match is a question of life or death; she tears her garments if she thinks of not having a certain guy, she herself determines it. And instead that guy takes the whole thing lightly and chooses someone else.

Instead, there is another guy who is extremely in love with her and she says: "This guy bores me, I would like the other and the other instead goes off with someone else." What a fix! Then the thing can get even more complicated: a third who enters, a fourth who enters, according to the capacity for endurance, and above all, the intelligence of the girl herself.

## Gladness[3]

Second step of our going deeper. From freedom from things, which poverty engenders, a feeling is born that is possessed only by the poor, that is, by those who don't place the hopes of their lives in determined things that they have chosen. One can place hope for one's life in a determined thing that one is given by God. If someone enters Gruppo Adulto he must hope for the happiness of his life from Gruppo Adulto, inasmuch as God has given him this vocation and insofar as he is at the mercy of the modality God uses and with which God uses things.

From this freedom from things, which is born from the certainty that God Himself fulfills everything, another characteristic of a person who is poor arises, which is gladness, of which the figure of Saint Francis is the emblem in the history of Christianity. Gladness finds its Magna Carta, its statute, in the gospel: "Blessed are the poor in spirit," blessed. Remember what Mauriac says in his *Life of Jesus*[4] – another book that is useful for you to read – remember the page on the Beatitudes, where Jesus, on the hill, says "Blessed ... blessed ..." Meanwhile all the people arrive and the last to arrive are the lame, the mentally retarded, the old, and since they arrive at the end they are at the back and strain their ears because they don't hear well. The only word they hear is a word that Christ repeats now and then with a raspy voice, raising his voice: "Blessed..." and they hear "Blessed ... blessed ... blessed ..." This pulls them in even more, makes them stretch forth with all their souls, but they don't hear the rest. Mauriac describes that page from the gospel thus.

From freedom from things – that comes from the certainty that God fulfills – a condition of gladness: it is here that faith gives birth to gladness. Faith does not give birth to gladness *immediately*, but *mediate-ly*: from faith, hope is born; gladness is in hope because gladness cannot be earned and lived if not in the certainty of a future. It is only a distortion that can give birth to a gladness and a joy from something that you have in hand in the present ... and tomorrow? A feeling is true when it responds to all of time's questions: it explains the past, clarifies the present, and assures the future.

The condition of gladness has its roots in faith: it is this attitude with which Saint Paul lived and which he described in a passage of the first letter to the Corinthians,[5] which Guido will now read.

*What I mean, brothers, is that the time has become limited, and from now on, those who have wives should live as though they had none; and those who mourn as though they were not mourning; those who enjoy life as though they did not enjoy it; those who have been buying property as though they had no possessions; and those who are involved with the world as though they were people not engrossed in it. Because this world as we know it is passing away.*

The substance of the world is not in what you see. The consistency of life, the happiness that the future holds for us, is not in what is seen. The visage of this world is passing, the consistency of our contentedness is not in what is seen; this is the description that is motivated by gladness. Gladness is something that exists because it rests on something that remains, even if the visage of this world, what appears now, passes.

One of the more vivid impressions that I have had in these two months was my visit to a bishop who was gravely ill, who, when he saw me, after an instant of emotion, sat down and said: "Time is growing short." Nevertheless, deep down, his expression was glad. Glad doesn't mean that one cheerfully says "I'm dying," that wouldn't be true, not even Saint Paul said that. Read this passage again.

*What I mean, brothers, is that the time has become limited, and from now on, those who have wives should live as though they had none ...*

It means that hope cannot be placed in the fact that one has a wife, one has a fiancé. Gladness is not derived from that; contentedness, which is more or less passing, is derived from that, but not gladness, because gladness rests on a possession whose perspective never ends.

*and those who mourn as though they were not mourning; those who enjoy life as though they did not enjoy it ...*

Those who enjoy, as if they didn't enjoy, doesn't mean they're there to cry, to cry because they won seven million in the lottery. One who cries because he's won seven million in the lottery is an idiot – that has nothing to do with the Christian subject. But gladness cannot have seven million dollars as its motive, it cannot; it doesn't follow. One can be content, but not happy, because that victory doesn't get rid of all the obstacles that arise to put the certainty of peace and the prospect of happiness in doubt.

*those who have been buying property as though they had no possessions.*

Imagine the young ladies on Fifth Avenue: on that street, there can be nervous contentedness, but not gladness; gladness for being on Fifth Avenue – no! Nervous contentedness, yes.

He who has, as if he did not have; one is free, and this freedom brings with it the seed of gladness: "Here is perfect gladness."[6] It's beautiful to have nice clothing, but one who has Christian faith and hope, deep, deep down would not be disturbed even if he had sackcloth instead of nice clothes; but it isn't convenient to go around wearing sackcloth!

There is no more beautiful formula for happiness than this: he who has, as if he did not have. Whether one has or doesn't have is equal ... but having something that lasts for eternity ... no, this cannot be equal! If you have something that lasts for eternity, then love, man's love for woman, love for a companion, love for parents, love for the sun that rises ...

As I described in the first volume of the School of Community[7] – I had read a book on Franciscan life where every chapter began with a design. In one of the designs at the beginning was a $Q$ – "Quando," the chapter began like that. That $Q$ had a little bird as a tail and inside was the outline of Saint Francis in front of the sun coming out: the symbol of the human sensitivity of our people, of our race, in front of nature's most beautiful subject: this is gladness. And the $Q$ introduced a sentence at the feet of Saint Francis: "Quid animo satis?" What can satisfy the soul? In fact, the expression of gladness is precisely in this question – "What can satisfy the soul?" – because the relationship between Saint Francis and the most beautiful phenomenon of nature was an eternal view, a perspective of the eternal, a sign of the eternal.

So, in true love, gladness exists inasmuch as possession is missing. It's not for naught that when speaking of virginity, we will say that it is poverty, that it is poverty at its extreme level, and it is for this that in dedicating oneself to God in virginity one must also give one's money, because without poverty, purity of dedication does not exist. In a love relationship, an affective relationship, the prospect of the eternal renders it happy and, while it renders it happy, it makes it free from conditions: the more this detachment exists within it, the more it becomes happy. This is not meant to exhaust the observation and the description of every moment. The initial period can be one of greater contentedness, but it has to do with contentedness, not with gladness; gladness is permanent.

Third step in the deepening of our discussion. Freedom doesn't only cause gladness; freedom in relationships doesn't only cause gladness. What does freedom in relationships mean? That the relationship rests on something permanent; that is, on the divine that remains. Not only does freedom cause gladness, but it makes you discover that you are deprived of nothing, you lack nothing, you lack nothing because everything is yours. How is it that everything is yours? Because you have what you need, you have everything that is necessary for you. Before going back to these sentences, let's listen to a chapter of the book published by Il Sabato, *Un avvenimento di vita cioè una storia*, which everyone should read.[8] There's a paragraph that explains this well.

*We need to become poorer or, rather, certain of some great things. If you are certain of some great things, then everything rests on the great things, everything develops from the great things, everything is a comment on the great things. Just as in a great work of music, everything is a comment on the principal theme or principal themes.*

*One who is poor is one who is certain of some great things (for which he constructs a cathedral even if he lives in a hovel, being a hundred times more a man in this way than he who has as an ultimate horizon in a comfortable apartment). Why is being poor being certain? Because certainty involves the abandonment and the overcoming of the self: "I am little, I am nothing, the 'true and great thing' is Another."*

*And this poverty makes us full, free, active, alive, because the law of man – the stable dynamism of that natural mechanism that is called man – is love, that is, the affirmation of Another as the meaning of the self.*

This is another way of expressing the essence of the question; because poverty is here, it can also be defined with this phrase: the affirmation of Another as the meaning of the self. The affirmation of Another as the meaning of the self doesn't mean to give fifty cents to the common fund, but to give everything, all of yourself to the common fund. But you give "all of yourself to common fund" by giving yourself to whomever the Lord puts in front of you – one, two, three, four, five, six – by obeying, obeying God, giving yourself therefore to another, as we'll see when we talk about charity: you can't be poorer than this! In love it is as if one died to oneself or as if one wanted to disappear in order to affirm an other.

*If it isn't easy to find people who are certain among us it is because there is no poverty. Poverty is a very adult conquest.*

*To be certain of some great things: this is faith. The word faith describes the essential relationship with "'something else" apart from us, apart from our opinions, our projects, the results of our actions: an Other, greater than everything that we can conceive and construct, on which our ultimate being depends, our destiny.*

*The people who built the church of Saint Ambrose in Milan were poor because they were certain of some great things, greater even than the work that they were capable of completing. Only the relationship with this "something other" allows the building of great and beautiful works, allowed them to build unceasingly and to surpass themselves even in the beauty of what they created.*

*Faith is certainty of a "great Presence" that allows the building of my relationship with reality, of my work and of my involvement in society, that allows my work to become something useful and "beautiful" before my eyes. Beautiful, because if it doesn't become a work of art, man's accomplishments are not human. The touch of art introduces an ideal reverberation into the mechanical manipulation of the real: "art that is the grandchild of God" Dante said, since true beauty is derived only from the One who saves beauty, the One who doesn't fear time, death, and pain.*

Thank you. Whoever has a Bible with him should go to Psalm 132, since we're speaking about people who live in hovels and build the Cathedral of Milan.

I'm not talking about the joke about the American in the taxi who passes the Pirellone[9] and says: "How much time did it take you to make that?" "A few years." "Phew, it would take us a week." Then he passes something else, where the government offices are: "How much time did it take you to build this thing here?" "Ah, some six months at least." "It would take us three days." Then the taxi goes through the square in front of the Duomo and the American says: "What's that thing there?" – the Cathedral – and the taxi driver says: "Oh, I don't know, it wasn't there this morning."

People who, living in hovels, built the church of St. Ambrose, lived with a spirit that reflects what Psalm 132 says:

*O Lord, remember in David's favour*
*all the hardships he endured;*
*how he swore to the Lord*
*and vowed to the mighty one of Jacob,*
*"I will not enter my house*
*or get into my bed;*
*I will not give sleep to my eyes*
*or slumber to my eyelids,*
*until I find a place for the Lord,*
*a dwelling place for the Mighty One of Jacob."*

It is David's purpose to create the temple of the Lord: "I will not be in peace until I will have constructed the house of the Lord." I cannot live in a house of hard wood or good wood when the house of the Lord is made of branches. This, described in Psalm 132, is a poverty of spirit; but wherever we see poverty of spirit exemplified, we feel within it a fluttering and a breath of gladness. A psalm like that can only be uttered in gladness. Like the passage we read earlier.

## 2 POVERTY, LAW OF THE DYNAMIC OF KNOWLEDGE

Let's add a final observation. We have established a premise and three steps to deepen it, now let's make a final, interesting observation: nevertheless people live without thinking of these things.

Poverty belongs to a dynamic law of knowledge, to a law of the dynamic of knowledge: to know something, a detachment is necessary. If I put a famous book here in front of my eyes, if one were born with a book stuck here, think of what the world would be! "Coki, where are you, Coki? Carlo, how is your strength?" It would be terrible. To know something it is necessary to have a detachment; it is this detachment that allows us to see things and therefore allows us to use them; because if I am born with a book stuck here, I might use Carlo as a shovel, and that would be a little improper! Is it clear? That detachment allows us to use things, but above all it allows us to enjoy them, to enjoy them more. Remember a comparison that rightly became famous from the School of Community,[10] an ingenious paradigm that reveals man's stupidity: to know a painting we don't have to look with our eyes a millimetre away. Then we would say: "What dots there are here!" and moving: "What a dot!" In a day and a half, breaking your back, you make everything move – if it is small – you make everything move, but: dot and dot and dot and dot … all that you've seen are dots, you can't enjoy it. If somebody comes and takes you by the collar and pulls you back a metre: ah, you see the painting! Without this detachment you can't know it, and thus you can't use it, nor can you enjoy it.

Beyond this comparison of the painting, this applies to everyone: between mother and child, between a boy and a girl, between a man and a woman, it works for whomever.

If you get too close, you can't see. Without a certain detachment, you don't know, you don't use, and you don't enjoy; the more the detachment is appropriate, that is, proportioned, the more you know, use, and enjoy.

Cardinal Giovanni Colombo, when he taught us Italian, used to say that to translate a figure or a view into poetry you need to have a certain detachment, without which it becomes neither a poem nor a painting; it doesn't become art. In that way, a mother who sees her child in a possessive way – without detachment within, without some detachment within, precisely within the relationship – can neither know nor have useful suggestions for the child, nor educate him nor enjoy him: she cannot enjoy her child. A man cannot enjoy a woman if not from a certain distance; otherwise he can enjoy her, but in the purely instinctive sense of the term. A mother who has never known a moment in which she gazes at her baby and, gazing at it from a metre or two or three's distance, thinks of its destiny: "Who knows what destiny this baby of mine will have." A woman who hasn't done this has never enjoyed being a mother, never; she can never have been a valid educator, never; she doesn't know the creature she has there. But this example, of the mother and the baby, is the paradigm for everything; because everything, for each one of us, for man, everything is like a baby who is born from the womb, everything.

Poverty belongs then to the dynamic of knowledge, for which a detachment is necessary to see things and then to use them and enjoy them more. Now you understand how one can speak of a detachment that is intelligent and full of affection. Without this detachment there would be no such intelligence and affection.

Thus, the phrase Saint Francis left us and that Nino Salvaneschi wrote as the summary of his book on Saint Clare, "After God and the firmament, Clare."[11] It's difficult to conceive of a loving exaltation greater than this. But think of the detachment there was, from the metric point of view, decimal metric. In fact it isn't a question of measurement, but ultimately of contextual company – the object, Clare, in Francis's eyes, was placed in the great company of the universe – it isn't a question of measurement but of company and, ultimately, of love; that is, of the abandonment of self, of the gift of self. It is better to say abandonment of self because it clarifies the idea of a gift. In a gift one always reserves the right to be esteemed, because one has given something, the right to gratitude, and this makes one lose everything; while in abandonment of self, no, it is pure. The abandonment of self: the more one loves the more one abandons oneself, and affirms only the other.

Meditate well on this beautiful lesson among yourselves because these are things that you don't hear anywhere and yet they constitute what we are called to live every day. Vocation is built from these factors.

Now I have to go to the Baptism of a nephew ... but the greatest thing is our eyes and our heart, which look at these things, our eyes and our heart, for the way in which they look at these things and love them: here you see "the new creature" that Baptism creates.

# 3  Trust

## THE PATH FROM FAITH TO TRUST

Up until now, what has been the path that our awareness and our thought have been provoked to fulfill?

### Faith

In our experience, there is something that comes from beyond it: unforeseeable, mysterious, but within our experience. If it is unforeseeable, not immediately visible, mysterious, with what instrument of our personality do we grasp this Presence? With that instrument called faith. Let's call this instrument "faith," to use a term that does not lead back to and is not exhausted by the concept of reason, because the comprehension of experience in its immediately experiential factors belongs to reason – it is reason that perceives our experience in its immediate factors – but in experience we feel the breath or the tremor or the consequences of a Presence that cannot be explained, that is surprising: a surprising encounter; therefore it is something beyond reason that can intuit and understand, and we call this faith, which is an intelligence of reality, an intelligence of experience.

Listen: if you don't understand something I'm saying, you should raise your hand and say: "I didn't understand this sentence." It's better to do that, because *drinking in* things or affirming things without our reason having illuminated them, so that our freedom must adhere to them, is unworthy of God, of Jesus and of ourselves, and it is unworthy of our friendship, and it is unworthy of the world's history.

I said that faith is a form of knowledge that is beyond the limit of reason. Why is it beyond the limit of reason? Because it grasps something that reason cannot grasp: reason cannot perceive "the presence of Jesus among us," "Christ is here now," the way it perceives that you are here. Do you understand? Yet, it cannot *not* admit that He is here. Why? Because there is a factor within, a factor that decides about this companionship, certain outcomes of this companionship, certain resonances of this companionship, a factor so surprising that if I don't affirm something else I don't give reason to the experience, because reason is to affirm experiential reality according to all the factors that make it up, all of the factors. There can be a constitutive factor, of which we only feel a reverberation, of which we feel the fruit, of which we even see the consequences, but we aren't able to see this factor directly. If I say: "So it doesn't exist," I am mistaken, because I eliminate something of the experience – this is no longer reasonable.

Faith is an act of the intellect, the catechism says. It's an act of knowledge that grasps the Presence of something that reason would not know how to grasp, but yet that reason has to affirm, otherwise something within experience would be lost, eliminated, something that experience *indicates*; therefore in some undeniable way it is within it. It is unexplainable, but it is within it. Now, of course, there is a capacity to understand within me, to know a level of reality that is greater than the usual; and I am obliged by reason to admit it. If I did not admit it, I would not affirm all the factors that make up my experience.

This thing is the supportive nucleus of the entire conception of knowledge and of the understanding of reality from the Christian point of view; the entire nucleus of Christian intelligence is here. It is necessary to understand this. It isn't necessary to understand *how* Christ is here; it is necessary to understand that one is *obliged to affirm* that there is something else here, because we aren't able to simply explain what is here by investigation, analysis, or examination of our reason.

When John and Andrew (we must always keep the first chapter of John's gospel before us, from verse 35 onward: then you understand everything, the whole problem of intelligence is there; while the entire moral problem is within the twenty-first chapter, from verses 15 to 18), when John and Andrew watched that man speak, they felt there was something exceptional there. They were not able to realize – they did not understand how; that is, their reason was not capable of grasping it – however, to be reasonable, they were obliged to say: "There is something else here." Why? Because to be reasonable means to affirm reality according to the totality of its factors, and if one of these factors is exceptional, it is necessary to say that it's there, even if one doesn't understand how. Do you understand or not? Be careful, because without knowing these things, you're not able to walk the roads of this "evil" world, Jesus says,[1] without being a slave of what surrounds you; it is as if they would tear out our eyes and our heart.

## Freedom

We said that the object of this faith, this Presence, that is irreducible to all normal factors, this exceptional Presence that faith grasps and affirms, empowers our freedom. Why? Because freedom can recognize it or not recognize it, that is, freedom can be sincere with itself or not.

How many people had heard Jesus? They stood there with their mouths agape listening to Him speak, but they went home, ate their fried eggs and forgot Him. The day after they cried out: "Crucify Him, crucify Him," and the day before they wanted to make Him king because He had given out free bread.

What difference is there between the apostles who followed Him and all the rest of the people? The rest of the people used their freedom badly; they didn't recognize what they had seen, because one who feeds five thousand people with a little bread is something that belongs to the world beyond, and everyone said: "He is something that belongs to the world beyond," to the extent that they wanted to make Him king, and He fled from them. Three days later they shouted: "Kill Him, kill Him," repeating what was then the equivalent of the press, television, and schoolteachers said.

So, this object that faith perceives can be recognized or not: freedom. Only in recognizing the object is freedom fulfilled.

## Obedience

Why can freedom not recognize Him? Because an effort is needed to recognize Him; it is necessary to adopt as a criterion not what you see, but what is. And what is is greater than what you see: it's called obedience, because the criterion of your affirmation is not what you see, but something that is within your present experience, yet is greater than your criteria, so much so that you wouldn't be able to explain it.

The doctors of the temple, in front of the boy whose name was Jesus of Nazareth and who was twelve years old, had already said: "But how does He manage to answer in this way? How does He manage to know these things?" And they didn't understand how he managed to know them, so they denied Him. Instead, no – the question remains paramount: "How does He manage to know these things?" That question would have brought them to the conclusion: "There is something there that we don't understand." And if He, instead of being twelve, was thirty-three, or thirty-two, or thirty-one, or thirty, and said: "I know these things because I am the Son of God," reason is obliged to say yes; that is, reason is obliged to affirm faith, and freedom must accept affirming faith, and accept that faith be affirmed.

Faith, therefore, brings knowledge of the truth of things, that truth for which man is made, that truth that man walks towards – freedom – that truth that cannot be discovered through analyses carried out by our own criteria, that is not automatically recognizable, but one that is only accepted; to adhere in this way to the criterion of Another, of the Mystery – the obedience of faith, faith as obedience.

## Hope

So we saw that this truth that faith makes us know is beyond what reason can understand when analysing its experience – reason can understand only that there is something else, or, as Pär Lagerkvist says in that famous poem: there is no answer to the voice that cries out; but why, then, do we have the voice that cries out?[2] And this is an open question. The only way to close this question is to say that there is something else: this is the entire foundation of *The Religious Sense*. The truth that faith makes us understand is a man, a man who sat down and ate together with others, who walked and plucked the ear from a stalk of wheat, and who sat down to eat the grain of wheat together with his own. That man was God, that is, the truth: "I am the Way, the Truth and the Life."[3]

And then we saw that certainty for the future is also founded on this truth. Even the future is certain with Him, therefore faith becomes hope, inasmuch as it no longer has to do with the surprise of a Presence, the surprise of an event – event: something present – but rather with the consequence of what one awaits in the end, of what one awaits deep down: faith becomes hope.

## Poverty

Yet if happiness, justice, truth, and beauty are beyond what we can see, what we can see and touch, what do they have to do with us? They have to do with us only to the degree that God makes us "find them at our feet" and we must use them for our work. And this is poverty: using reality exclusively for the work that we must do with it. We are called to carry out a task: this is a concept that you must add to last time's discussion. Poverty is not automatic. It is not like one in the gutter who's got lice and a few measly rags hanging from him. Poverty is the *use* of reality according to the destiny that, with certainty, is proposed to us and awaits us.

Poverty is our initiative. If it is not our initiative, it is not poverty. Poverty is an act of freedom; it is not submission, but a taking hold in order to walk, a grasping in order to construct, a grasping in order to respond to the vocation of God.

Therefore, man is no longer attached to things: today he must use them, and tomorrow they will no longer be here, tomorrow he must use others. For this reason, the more you are interested in a person, the more you care about treating that person as an instrument for the common path towards your destiny and his or her destiny, the more you care about poverty in the relationship: poverty in the relationship is the truth of the relationship.

The opposite of the truth of the relationship is that which proposes itself as a lie in the relationship. In the relationship with the thing that you like or the person you love, it would be a lie if the person or thing were to tell you, or you treated the person or thing as if it said: "I am enough for you. I am everything you live for," and this is not true.

The more you love, the easier, lighter, and freer the relationship becomes. And the time and space into which the relationship always translates are not pretexts. You don't demand to see the person after an hour, you don't demand to see her every minute, you don't demand to have the thing here, there, or wherever. Time and space are conquered, in poverty they are conquered: one is free, not in the ethical sense we mentioned earlier, but in the sense of lightness: "The unbearable lightness of being" like that book of Adelphi.[4] The truth of this sentence is exactly what I'm saying, aside from what the book says!

Poverty makes you use things for destiny, and this is using things as if you weren't using them, having them as if you did not have them, possessing them as if you did not possess, as that beautiful passage from Saint Paul[5] says.

1  TRUST IS TO ENTRUST YOURSELF TO SOMEONE

Now, at this point, we find we have to give up the possession of things – poverty – to move quickly, lightly, freely, towards destiny. And the more I love a person, the more I want that person with me on the path towards destiny; therefore what I'm saying applies all the more to this person: there is a detachment, according to our definition of virginity (which is a possession with a detachment within it). It's necessary to detach ourselves from things, because they are light; we use them and they disappear, we use them and they wear out, much more quickly than some battery, because everything is like a charged battery!

On the one hand, one should live this poverty; that is, this provisional use of things and this use of relationships with persons, literally exhausted by the tension towards the common destiny. I cannot linger with this person, if I linger I treat her badly, I lie: she isn't made to have me, neither am I made to have her, but she and I are made for a common destiny, to have something infinite in common. So then, we have to let go of things, be free from people. The first impression is that this poverty is a big trap! We remain as if suspended over an abyss, over a void: the final word should be void, *suspended over a void*.

Instead, the result that poverty is destined to bring is the opposite. Poverty is not destined to leave us suspended over a void, but poverty that is born from hope is destined to establish, to exalt, to enlarge, to fill the entire world, so that our eyes see avidly, with trust. The result of poverty that is born from hope is called trust, which is the opposite of being suspended over a void. Trust is the opposite of being suspended over a void: it is being *suspended over a fullness*.

The object discovered by faith – for Andrew and John, it was Jesus, that night – the object discovered by faith is like that young man Father Emmanuel told me about yesterday. A young man from Brescia, a university professor, sent him a letter saying he was a Buddhist (in fact, he enclosed the book of Zen, a book you don't see around anymore) and that his fiancée, who lives in Guastalla Square, invited him to Father Emmanuel's Mass at Saint Peter's in Gessate. "I've been coming to this Mass for a while now," he says in the letter, "and I have to admit there's something here I don't understand. So I'm sending you this book, read it, because I'm reading it too, I meditate on it and I like it, and I'm also sending you one hundred dollars as an offering for your movement." I looked at the book and I understood once again something I've understood for a while, but yesterday I understood it really well. It is a wise man's book, full of wise observations, wise reflections; but what a burden the sage has! How burdensome life is, if you had to follow wisdom: extremely burdensome! It's the opposite of the "unbearable lightness of being." The life of a sage is unsustainable, so much so that it is impossible to find a sage who carries out what he says, what he thinks. All the sentences were extremely beautiful – apart from the fact that the most beautiful ones were things that we say too: they coincided!

The truth we are made to discover from faith – Jesus, for John and Andrew – this truth, which is that man, sustains the weight of our entire future, until it arrives at destiny. Therefore Christian hope does not finish in a "Let's hope!" or better yet, in dialect, "*Sperem!*" but ends in a certainty that embraces everything.

The object discovered by faith sustains all of life's weight, all of our future, until it arrives at completeness, at the final fulfillment of God's design, which is our destiny. It is the object discovered by faith that sustains our entire future, it is the object discovered by faith that sustains all of the unknown of hope, because hope is full of the unknown.

It is that man Jesus they heard speak, that John and Andrew looked in the face, it is Jesus who carried the entire weight of their future, right up to their destiny. The new word that we must use is trust. That man created a trust in them that Peter voiced in the sixth chapter of Saint John when he said: "Master, even we don't understand what you say, but if we go away from you, where shall we go? You alone have the words that explain life." These words carry the weight of life, according to the trajectory that goes on to finish at destiny, that is, at our fulfillment. Hope lasts until fulfillment. This is introduced by the concept of trust.

Poverty, therefore, is not an abandoning, but is defined by the road towards having, towards the truth of having. Trust, in fact, comes from the Latin verb *fidere, fidere se alicui*, to entrust yourself to someone. Trust is entrusting yourself to someone.

Trust, therefore, has hope within it, hope as fulfillment; that is, it has poverty within it as a rule of life. Even if one doesn't want to, one is obliged to let go. The psalms say this well when they speak of the rich: "I had so much envy for the rich, so much anger toward them, but then I understood, Lord: in the morning they were that way and in the evening they were there no longer."[6] It is poverty in the positive sense; it is the positive sense of poverty: trust: *fidere se alicui* (entrusting yourself to someone).

## 2  THE COROLLARIES OF TRUST

### a) Abandonment

What is the first corollary, the first consequence of this entrusting yourself to someone? Another way of saying the same thing: it is the word abandonment. Abandonment brings to mind again the word poverty, as if one had to deprive oneself of something; but instead, it is not a deprivation. Abandonment is like a child with its mother, it is security. Read *Un avvenimento di vita cioè una storia*, pages 35 and 36.[7]

*You speak of "a profound optimism in front of existence and of history which the Christian arrives at by means of the awareness of Christ's resurrection."*
John and Andrew, while they were listening to Him speak, could not have a fear of life or a question as to whether life was negative or positive. The impulse they felt towards life when that man spoke was naturally full of optimism, an optimism that rested on Him; the point of the entire future rested on His face, on His mouth, on His nose, on His eyes; it rested there.

*Which signifies a zest and a love for the involvement with time and with space.*
A zest and a love: they come only from this optimism, only from this trust that is manifested as abandonment. John and

Andrew abandoned themselves to that man and, in fact, that evening they went home and were different; they were different because they had completely relied on what they had seen; and the next day they went back to see Him, then they went back to see Him again, then they went back to see Him again, then they followed Him.

*A zest and a love for the involvement with time and*
*with space ...*
"A zest and a love in time and in space" means work: from sweeping the house, to a man's love for a woman or a man's love for his companion on the path; because if it isn't work it is deceit. It is work, it is the path to destiny.

*That even in the brevity and the poverty of the instant,*
*they would not be found in any other human position.*
This book also speaks of the history of the Movement as *ingenuous boldness.*[8] The Movement matured and walks onward with ingenuous boldness: *ingenuous*, which means without anything that intrudes upon it, without anything that does not come from the origin, without anything arti-ficial ... in fact, he who is artificial doesn't derive satisfaction from the Movement, doesn't live it. Ingenuous *boldness* is security that deep down makes for abandonment: only when a baby – Psalm 130 – is within its mother's arms is it bold, abandoned.

The sign of abandonment is as if one had all one's sources of pride dried up. He no longer grows proud, it becomes impossible to become proud because nothing is his, and yet everything becomes his if nothing is his. If you are the

Lord and therefore everything is yours, if I recognize this, it all becomes mine: I follow you and everything becomes mine! As Monsignor Galbiati, the great biblical scholar who previously had been the head of the Ambrosian Library, said from the terrace of the seminary at Venegono, where there is a spectacular view of all the Alps – from Monviso to Monte Rosa – on a beautiful night: "Look, this is all mine. For now I leave it there, because ..." Anyone who spoke like that was a child, anyone who has met Monsignor Galbiati knows he is like a child.

### b) I can do all things in the One who is my strength

Second corollary. This optimism determines every reawakening, every revival of consciousness, so that life's motto, life's formula becomes what Saint Paul said: "I can do all things, I am capable of all things together with Him in whom lies my strength [my reason for being, my strength, my substance]."[9]

This means total confidence even in front of all of one's own weaknesses. I am so weak that I don't say: "I would mess up every minute," but I do mess up every minute. If I observe myself, I lose heart: every minute I mess up. Instead: "I am capable of all things together with Him in whom lies my strength." If I recognize that my strength is in Him, none of my weaknesses can stop me.

In the little book *Dalla fede il metodo* – watch out, since it's truly a crime that the majority of you don't read the texts we bring out; those who don't read these texts commit a crime, a crime against themselves and also against humanity because, if they are baptized and, even more, have a vocation, they have a duty to work towards the world's well-being, towards a better humanity – at a certain point that text says more or less the following: "It isn't necessary to cultivate plans of perfection, but to look Christ in the face,"[10] and this is the most beautiful corollary to John 21, to Jesus who says to Simon: "Simon, do you love me?" and Simon responds: "Yes Lord, you know that I love you."

Don't daydream and aim for perfection, but look Christ in the face: if one looks Christ in the face, if one looks someone one loves in the face, everything is straightened out, everything falls into place, and the hair is placed in a certain way, and the button is buttoned, and he is ashamed of his dirty shoes and says: "Excuse me for being so sloppy." The source of being moral is loving someone, not fulfilling laws.

Pardon me, but can we imagine the origin of morality conceived in a simpler way? Not projects of perfection, but looking Christ in the face, looking someone in the face! Extremely simple, extremely easy ... but extremely uncomfortable; extremely uncomfortable because you can't follow yourself anymore. Happiness is to follow Another.

Sure, to look Christ in the face and not make all sorts of plans to be perfect means that you look Christ in the face truly desiring the good, truly desiring to be true, truly desiring to love: "desiring you truly, O Lord."

Now it is Holy Week. On Holy Thursday, Good Friday, Holy Saturday, Easter, in these four days if you go inside without simply looking Christ in the face, but rather preoccupied about your sins or about perfection or about things to meditate on, you come out tired and pick up where you left off. Looking Christ in the face, instead, you change. But to change, you must truly look Him in the face, with the desire for good, the desire for truth: "I am capable of all things, Lord, if I am with you who are my strength." It is a you that dominates, not things to respect.

Try to think of how no one, no one, understands these things: no one thinks of them and no one understands them. Instead, this is the only true revolution in the world: faith as knowledge, and charity – looking Christ in the face – as morality.

The first letter of John, first chapter, speaks of God's faithfulness: "If we say 'We are without sin,' we deceive ourselves, and the truth is not in us. If we acknowledge our sins, He is faithful and just and will forgive our sins and cleanse us from every wrongdoing."[11] It is in looking Him in the face that one feels this purifying, cleansing strength; it isn't like going to confess: "one, two, three, four, five, six, seven, eight, nine, ten, twelve sins: I said all twelve of them." But when I look Him in the face, He, who is faithful and just, forgives.

It's the famous case of the child who breaks something and looks at his mother, and his mother takes his face in her hands and kisses him right away, forgiving him – everything he did disappears. But if one were there with the awareness of being capable of repeating the mistake a hundred thousand times, but without the intention of repeating it, this means to truly desire to please Him, to follow Him.

## 3  THE GREATEST BANQUET IN THE HISTORY OF THE HOUSE

Fourth and final observation. It is from this forgiveness, from this power that comes from within me, it is from this ability to do everything together with the One who establishes my strength, with He who is faithful to me – "You are faithful to me. I am extremely weak, you are faithful to me: I am capable of everything" – it is from this profound and simple trust that the greatest banquet in the history of the house is born: the prodigal son. Which means to say, the continuous outcome of this new life, which could be so slovenly, so impoverished, so cowardly, so mean, so ugly, so dirty ... the outcome is a great feast. As I said before, it is the feast that qualifies every reawakening, every morning, every time you say "O God," every time you look at Him and say "O God, forgive me." It is a feast, a feast occurs. Trust is a state of the soul such that from whatever position you're in, you have a feast. If you have trust, a capacity for victory together with the One who is your strength is born, even from all your weaknesses; a capacity for victory is born that is the boldness of those seven or eight disciples who were the first to have followed Him. There were seven or eight of them, and they already had and repeated the awareness of conquering the world, of being the new Jewish people: that which would conquer the world, because it was with Him.

## Mission and gladness

The greatest banquet in the history of the house comes from trust. The outcome of trust is always a feast. Think of a great feast like the one the father of the prodigal son held: everything turns upside down, the entire house was turned upside down.

Everything turns upside down, and this is called mission, making a mission of one's very life. One gets up in the morning for a mission, and one goes to school for a mission, and one sweeps the house for a mission and one has house meetings[12] for a mission. The word mission enhances everything in the same way that the soul of Christ, the one who was sent, enhanced things. Everything turns upside down, and this is mission.

Everything is turned upside down, even what is within us, everything within us turns upside down. And this feast, if it turns upside down everything within us, what does it do? It makes us glad, the final consequence of trust is gladness. And not because you're standing there counting yesterday's mistakes and saying "O God, I didn't commit them." This is, first, a presumption, which means you are not keeping your eyes open; and second, this has nothing to do with it, nothing. You could have committed a hundred, the problem of your gladness does not depend on this.

Everything is turned upside down, even we ourselves, and this makes us glad. Everything is turned upside down and this makes our life surge with mission; everything is turned upside down in us and this makes us glad. So that if one were sad and degraded, trust is the optimism of every reawakening, and every reawakening becomes a feast.

## Generator of a people

As an immediate example, one sees this attitude of a feast in a child when he or she is with his or her mother and father. Yet it is a feast that, if it is seen first of all in the child, lasts even in the adult and makes the adult – you, you at this age – makes the adult the leader of a new history, a craftsman, a protagonist of a new history in the world, which means to say the creator of a people, the generator of a people: to create a people it is necessary to generate.

It is this that we read in today's midday prayer: "So, having sought your precepts, I shall walk in all freedom, because I seek your precepts, I shall proclaim your decrees to kings [that is, your plan, the plan you have for man's life, without fearing anything] without fear of disgrace. Your commands fill me with delight, and I love them deeply [in Your presence, Your commands are Your presence, which I love. And His presence goes to the left and you go to the left, goes to the right and you go to the right, sits down and you sit down; stops to eat and everyone stops to eat, performs a miracle and everyone was there with his mouth open]. And I stretch out my hands to your beloved commandments and meditate on your statutes."[13]

But the most beautiful comparison is that of this last psalm: "Happy are you who fear the Lord [who love the Lord], who walk in His ways. For you shall eat the fruit of your handiwork [the work we spoke about before:

poverty is using all of reality to create the path to destiny]; happy shall you be, and favoured. Your wife [because in God's plan there is one thing that is closer to you and there are other things that are farther away, and you reach the farther ones through the closer ones. It is an idea regarding marriage that no one understands; the idea of marriage is this: what is closer to you is more deeply a sign of everything], your wife shall be like a fruitful vine in the recesses of your home [a miracle]; your children like olive plants [after the wife, the children; and after the children, the children's children; and after the children's children, the children's children's children; and so from Abraham a people is born, which is the most powerful people on the earth today, even if it isn't the most politically powerful: the Jews]. Behold, thus is the man blessed who fears the Lord. The Lord bless you from Zion! [Make your life full of the Lord's feast, that mysterious place from which He dominates the world]. May you see the prosperity of Jerusalem [the prosperity of your people, of your movement, of your Church] all the days of your life; May you see your children's children [may you see this line that multiplies for a long time, for as long as possible]."[14]

The outcome of trust is that you become the origin of a people, through what is close to you, such as a matrimonial reality that generates something close to you – that comes from your house: your children – and something that is born of them, and something that is born still after, and that which is born after: "May you see for a time this generating of the people of God." Well, forty years ago, there were five of us: four kids, whom I met on the sidewalk on the Via Lamarmora, and myself, who went from home to school upset, upset because the Communists always rallied, the fascists always rallied and there were no traces of Catholics. But there were five of us: "Do you want to get together with me tomorrow at Via Statuto 2?" They said to me: "Yes," and so it began.

"May you see your children's children ...," but the line doesn't end where your eye reaches; the road is long. How long must it be? As long as God wants, who knows? "But of that day [the great feast of Christ, of the man Christ, will be from one end to the other: all the world will see and will say "It was true"] or hour, no one knows, neither the angels in heaven, nor the Son [not even Christ], but only the Father [the mystery of creation]."[15]

We'll see each other in two weeks. Take this passage by passage, word by word, sentence by sentence, look it in the face, ask the Madonna to make you understand, then speak of it among yourselves, but this is the last thing to do!

## 4  AWARENESS OF TIME

Every time we get together like this, willingly or unwillingly, we are struck by the awareness of time past, of the time that has passed, of time that passes. I say of time that has passed because this is also a summary of how we have behaved, of how we've used this time, aware of time past, and therefore aware of time that passes. The most important is this last thing: awareness of time that passes. The awareness of past time enlightens us, makes us shrewder;

time that passes can activate us in a more intelligent way. Time past is an experience that should make us more attentive to time that passes, aware of its meaning; meaning is the direction passing time takes, time being a mobilization of everything, of all that we see, of all that we feel. All that we see, all that we feel is the object or subject of a mobility that passes and filters everything – mountains, stars, faces – through something within us, awareness of destiny and freedom: now it becomes mobilization, awareness of past time that becomes awareness of time that passes. This mobilization of time that passes, this sense of time that passes – this interests us above all – what does it imply, what does it require of us? What do everything that has happened and everything that happens have to do with us?

Let's invoke the Spirit of Mystery that makes all things, because we must be alive; first, objective regarding the past and alive for the present, in order that everything in us proceeds, *proceeds*, goes forward towards what it's made for. Let's pray to the Holy Spirit: COME HOLY SPIRIT.

### a) Time does not belong to us

Briefly, before advancing into the mystery of the Lord, into the mystery of Christ, into His death and resurrection, let's try to clear our spirits of the imperatives with which we imaginatively and grudgingly codify our usual way of living. Our usual way of living is fixed on images to which we attribute the value of time; it is fixed on projects, on dreams, on expectations to which we attach life's value, the worth-the-trouble of living. I won't go into all this now, but being aware of past time means to understand first of all the factors with which to judge these images we fix, these phantoms in which our dream crystallizes, these physiognomies in which the worth-the-trouble of living crystallizes, or seems to crystallize. Because it is in the convergence of these observations that the right position from which to proceed is stabilized, it is on the basis of these discoveries and redis-coveries – because they must always become rediscoveries, but they must first be discovered – that our steps walk towards their end, the ultimate frontier.

This brief link will be underlined by our songs,[16] because all of our songs bring us back to the discovery and redis-covery of what we said: to judge the meaning of what we do; to establish the value of time; to judge how we exalt the thing on which we fix our self-esteem and the esteem of things.

In the past – I am speaking about last month; I am speaking about yesterday, first, and then of last month, and of two months ago, three months ago, of Advent before Christmas and of October when we started the path of Gruppo Adulto (we should at least be conscious of this) – what have we liked in these months, what has satisfied us, what has made us know and love more, what has made our life more satisfying? Let's say it in its most banal form: everything we liked – because, if we haven't liked any-thing, it will be hard to continue on this same path, because liking things is very important in making our relationship with people and things (which are the same) continue – what we liked does not belong to us, what we liked was not generated by us, was not decided by us, was not imag-ined by us, was not created by us. The fact that time was pleasing to us did not depend on us: it was ours and did not belong to us. It was ours and did not belong to us, and this is so true that it has passed. Yet if we don't think of these things, what are you weeping at, Dante said,[17] if you don't think of these things, at what are you laughing? What feeling do you have towards life? You are without fear, like a piece of wood, like a tree, you're dead!

And whatever displeased us in the past, what we did not like, what weighed on us, was not for us, that is, was not willed by us (it would be absurd!); even that did not belong to us. It is clearer still that it did not belong to us. What displeased us belonged to something else, something inevitable.

What we liked and what we didn't like, nothing belonged to us, nothing belonged to us, up until an hour ago, up until half an hour ago, up until what happened a minute ago.

Because our life, which began in our mother's womb, which was roughly hewn from it, which assumed its form when we were three years old, four, five, and the reflex feelings that were always more interesting, whether they were pleasing or displeasing, that we felt when we were elementary school age; and then our whole development: meetings and non-meetings, the content of work, the content of what we looked at, the content of the reflex of time, of our flesh, of our bone, of our temperament, of our viscera (in women this is made more evident, through the very cycle that happens in the female body): all of this was life, but it wasn't ours, *inevitable*. Our life belongs to Another – we'll put it that way to abbreviate the understanding – strange in itself, enigmatic, mysterious; we are used to calling it God, but we can't even call it God, we don't have the right to call it God if we don't perceive it in its elusive mystery.

Inevitability is in a way the most clarifying synonym of this fact that the thing does not belong to us and, above all, that from which all things derive does not belong to us: our life belongs to Another.

In this sense you understand why man's life is dramatic: if it did not belong to Another it would be tragic. Tragedy is when a building falls and all the stones and pieces of marble and pieces of wall crumble. Imagine it, look at the castle that crumbles: everything falls to pieces, until there is nothing more, there is only the unformed mass of bricks, stones, stone, there is nothing more.

All of life becomes nothing, is destined to become nothing, because of what we lived in the past, of what we lived up until an hour ago, up until five minutes ago; nothing is formed, nothing is constructed any longer. And this is tragic. Tragedy occurs because everything *corruit*, everything corrupts; it is as if all things fled from each other, they are no longer attached. Tragedy is the nothing of the finish line, the nothing, the nothing of what is.

While if everything belongs to Another, to something of Another, then this question is dramatic: it is dramatic because there is an I and a you, there's a proposal and a response, it is a dialogue. A year ago this was proposed to us: "Give me your life," and in October the response was: "I'll give it to you, here I am, I am present." All of this must surface in our response when our name shows up at the weekly gathering. The drama is in the free tension, in the free response to the free proposal between an I and a You.

For this reason man's life is dramatic, not tragic. Tragedy is made of atheism, drama is made of humanity, in which the I recognizes that everything that is belongs to You, even if this You veils itself in something enigmatic, obscures itself in something enigmatic, mysterious.

We must think of this when, for example, we sing "Prendi pure la mia vita" [Go Ahead, Take My Life] or when we say psalms in which this concept is developed: "I offer." But let's re-sing the simplest song, the most comprehensible: prendi pure la mia vita means I accept to be yours, I accept that I am not mine, I accept being possessed, I accept belonging to something of Another which You are, however this You is. Let's sing this song quickly and *sotto voce*, as if it were a thought that is developing within us. SONG: PRENDI PURE LA MIA VITA.

## b) The mystery is good

I recognize that I belong to you, recognize that time was not mine, didn't belong to me, just as up to today time does not belong to me, it isn't mine. Take my life, I accept that it doesn't belong to me, I recognize that it doesn't belong to me, I accept that it doesn't belong to me.

The song states the second fundamental category with which we judge the flow of past time, with which we become conscious of the past. What is it? "You gave your life to save me." What possesses our time died for us, presents itself to our eyes and to our heart as the place where our destiny is loved, where our happiness is loved, so much that He who possesses time dies for our time. But I don't want to stress this aspect of Holy Week, I want to stress that the Lord, He to whom time belongs, is good. This is so true that even before he dies for us, and then rises for us, he adds time to time, prolongs our time. "He is patient with you, not wishing that any should perish, but that all should come to repentance,"[18] Saint Peter says to the first Christians.

The Lord loves, this Mystery that time is made of – our past life up until now – wants our good, wants our happiness, loves our destiny. For this he has held us in a companionship that has as its one value, through everything – through playing and weeping together, through collaboration and help – that of recalling us to the goodness of destiny, the good end: being is good.

All of modern philosophy flees from this and therefore flees from the concreteness of being and directly denies, easily denies, the consistency of things and throws everything into the abyss of our dreams, into an abyss of dreams. And instead we are embraced. A companionship fastens around our waists, a companionship that continually recalls us to destiny, to the Mystery who makes things for our good, for our destiny of happiness. This Mystery is good, this enigmatic You is good. It takes us by the hand through this companionship. SONG: MI PRENDI PER LA MANO [You Take Me by the Hand].

Re-read the last stanza of the song.

*The storm surges on my path, even in the dark night,*
*You are near.*

You are near. How? If He is near, one perceives Him.
How is He perceived? Through the companionship, the
companionship in which He holds us, which we wouldn't
ever have chosen this way, never. In the previous stanza it
says: "I entrust myself to You only, oh Lord." You are the
only one who makes my life full of meaning, Lord, who
makes time full of meaning, in the history of the companionship in which you hide the intervention of Your
mystery, the Spirit.

### c) Sorrow, love for a present

The awareness of our past, after having discovered these
two fundamental points – that we don't belong to ourselves, that time doesn't belong to us, didn't belong to us;
and that He who gave it to us, gave it to us for our good –
has a third thing to tell us. It isn't a fundamental category,
it's a passing category, by its nature passing, in the sense that
by its nature it must be overcome, passed through.

"I entrust myself to You, O Lord." We haven't only
given our trust to Him, we have hoped, we have entrusted
ourselves to men: parents, teachers, friends, the girlfriend,
the boyfriend, the instance, the way in which things should
happen. We have entrusted ourselves to a vain hope: placing yourself in front of the future saying *let's hope* is sense-
less, is empty. Not entrusting ourselves to Him to whom
we belong, according to whatever modality, this is sin:
failing Him to whom we belong, and therefore failing the
certainty of His salvation; responding no, like a great

caprice, to the drama of dialogue between us and He who is time, who is in time, who is time as salvation.

The awareness of our past, a little or a lot, is like a great emptiness in which we've failed in the attack, like one who slides down a mountain, towards the chasm. This aspect of our past that has rejected the fact of recognizing its own belonging is called *evil*; that, above all, has said no to the proposal of good with which the presence of the Lord is identified, of He who is the master. Evil, and in fact if we now suspended our dialogue and every one of us were able to recollect himself and think of his past up to last night – let's fix on last night – until last night from last October: "My God, what emptiness!" The best of this emptiness was distraction, that is, the renunciation of intelligence and of love; the best, because the worst was the no. But the no is the most infantile aspect of an antithesis by which we have entrusted ourselves to something other that was not He; we hoped for good not from Him, not from the shadow of light He gives to our lives; we were not entrusted; and we hoped for our good not from the voice, the urging, the example, the perspective of the community, of the companionship in which He has placed us, because He has taken us by the hand in the companionship.

I am not being pessimistic, because it is true that in all the past days from October up until last night, how many lapses of forgetfulness, how many compromises of aban-donment, of resting on something that was not seen as His, how much hope that relied on something that we ourselves fixed or was promised to us by the first person who came along, by the first billboard we saw, or by the first commercial we saw on television: by human stories full of lies, except for the form in the photograph.

For this reason, in the end, *looking at the past,* we remain either ignobly immobile, or ashamed, or full of resentment – towards something or towards the person who obstructed what was the best, the good, the more just satisfaction – full of resentment, full of anger at ourselves, disappointed by ourselves; and *looking ahead,* confused, not knowing what to do; but the more correct word is shame. In front of what is ahead of us, shame, a sense of impotence; deep down – it is because we are not used to the right way – desperation. What can you expect from yourself? Desperation.

If this were the finish line, if today were the finish line, what prize would our time since October until last night have earned? What prize would it deserve? We could say, for the sake of clarity, that it would deserve a punishment. And in fact, in front of past time, in front of that which foresees the future, we're afraid. Who knows? What will happen? Who knows what will happen? We are afraid because the Mystery cannot be happy with us. Who will repair what we've destroyed or what we've allowed to sink into nothing?

This is truly the third important thing in the awareness we must have of past time and thus in the awareness we should have in the face of present and future time; this third thing is the most important, it is the strangest and most fascinating of all. Not terror, shame, or fear of our weakness and our evil – this is what it is to consecrate selfishness, this is what it is to make selfishness eternal, this is hell, making selfishness eternal – not shame over evil and fear of time, but *sorrow*.

In what way can we distinguish sorrow from fear? Fear is if the mountain falls on top of you, if the hills crush you, if the stars fall, if there's universal chaos; fear is what oppresses and suppresses you. Sorrow, instead, is the most concrete form of love for us. You cannot feel sorrow if you are not in front of a you, of a person, of a present person. Human drama therefore is sorrow in which lies the continuous recuperation of love; sorrow is love for something present. What is there to love that is present? The past taught us and will teach us evermore: what is present to love is what doesn't fade away. What doesn't fade away? The one who possesses everything.

It is the emergence, the becoming aware of sorrow, of a sorrow, that makes us look ahead of ourselves, glimpsing that Presence that gave us life, that made us move ahead, and that died for us: the Saviour: that Presence that assures us of our happiness at the end, that Presence in which the ultimate horizon lies; but it is *Presence* and it gives us the ultimate horizon.

Sorrow because I offended you, sorrow because I offend you; speaking this way, the offence is already redeemed, its aspect changes, and betrays – in the good sense of the word – documents a love that is present, regardless of the defect. In sorrow, stronger than the delusion of evil, the delusion of weakness, the shame at ourselves, is love.

When we gather together, we must always take up and renew these three things that we've said. "O Sweetness of Hidden Love." It is present, it takes me by the hand – this is so true that you are here, you, and you, and you; we wouldn't be together! Nevertheless it is hidden, because it reveals itself slowly, very slowly in passing time, so that the patience of His mercy is demonstrated, *"patienter agit propter vos,"*[19] it moves with patience, having mercy on us. SONG: O DOLCEZZA D'AMORE NASCOSTA (O Sweetness of Hidden Love).

## TRUST: ASSEMBLY

This Spanish song that Carmen sings for us every now and then is beautiful,[19] but the Beethoven concerto[20] we listened to before is certainly just as beautiful. What, you didn't like it? You know there's a special story for me about this concerto. When I was teaching in freshman year of high school (in my first year of high-school teaching), to demonstrate the existence of God, I would go from my house to the Berchet Lycée with a record player under my arm – back then, there weren't those small ones, there were those big ones with the trombone – I dragged this gramophone behind me and I made them listen to Chopin, Beethoven ... One of the first that I had them listen to was this Beethoven concerto. I had them listen to it to demonstrate how, when a musical genius – or an artist, anyway – has had the intuition of something beautiful, a beautiful melody, it's inevitable that he will bring it back so that this beautiful melody becomes a sort of refrain, a refrain for the whole piece; it's impossible for it not to come back; even more, coming back, it's bound to determine the thing we remember most in the piece. For example, for this reason, I used to bring Chopin, and go through the entire outline of the Les Adieux Waltz on the blackboard.

I had them listen to this Beethoven Concerto where there's the refrain, which I called the refrain "of the community," when the whole orchestra enters and always has the same melody, then the violin, which represents singularity, takes off three times and leaves for its destiny until, tired, it's taken back by the melodic theme of the entire orchestra (which closes out the piece). When we heard this piece, in that classroom, that is, where there was total silence, a girl who was in the first desk, here on the right, named Milena Di Gioia – I still remember her – suddenly started crying her eyes out, and wasn't able to stop. I let her go on a little, then I said: "You can see well the difference between one soul and another, one sensibility and another, between one heart and another." Those others certainly wouldn't have cried. Therefore, from that moment, this piece became more meaningful for me.

The longing that the fundamental theme generates, it's such longing, that for a sensibility like Milena's, it made her burst into tears – this longing is man's emblem of waiting for God.

*I wanted to recount something that happened to me today. While coming here, I was very "charged-up" for this moment, because I had the desire to be here with all of you, I had the desire to understand more. Then, along the road, I happened to see an accident in which a girl was killed. This fact upset me, because it changed my position. At that point, I began to ask myself: but why did this happen? And I also began to be a little afraid. But I realized that within this fear, I wasn't alone: I had a place to bring my question; I had the desire to come here because I had a place where I await a response.*

This statement providentially calls us back to precisely the three points we made before dinner.[21] Let's put ourselves in your place, witnessing that terrible scene: no one would know how to respond, because there's a question that presents itself, but no one would be able to respond. Moreover, everyone would be so stunned that even that same question wouldn't arise. Instead, we say: even this girl, like me, truly belongs to Christ, belongs to Another, belongs to the Mystery that makes things. We respond in this way, and in responding this way, one feels that it responds, understands that it responds, because it is an answer, it is the answer, the only answer. And in this answer, the heart, wounded though it may be, paradoxically finds ultimate repose.

Then you come here, and the companionship – second point of this evening – calls you back to destiny, that is, calls you back to this belonging.

So you understand – like that little girl if she would come back to life – you understand how the sole value of life is in adhering, accepting to adhere to Him to whom we belong. Sorrow begins to affirm itself, because sorrow exists only when one has love.

In the face of the dead little girl, it's a horrifying scene more than sorrow; sorrow is what her father and mother experience, something like a last ditch effort to give an answer to her no longer existing. For us, instead, it becomes sorrow when we think about the history of that life, about her father, her mother, about her other friends, about all the people there who don't understand. So you really understand that the only question of life is not to offend, not to sin, the only harm in life is sin. The force that allows you not to sin, that purifies you from sin, even to the point of taking it away from everything, as in the unique case of Mary, is another force, not our will.

*I was wondering: why did Fr. Gius, speaking about trust, speak about forgiveness? Reflecting on it, it came to mind that without this word, trust (that is, to say to Christ "You are my strength") would be an abstraction, it would be a future without a basis.*
It would be a prospect without an object and with no horizon; it would be an opening with no horizon, without content. There was a great philosopher – he became famous particularly in politics – Ernst Bloch, who put forth this concept, the concept of hope for him was this: a waiting at random.

Why is it, do you think, that without forgiveness there can't be trust? Because man is a sinner, and it's impossible for him not to err, not to make mistakes, and he's weak in the face of everything (his strength is in Another). In this way, none of our mistakes, none of our sins, none of our offences would be an objection to the vocation. If instead of committing ninety crimes, one would commit one hundred eighty – murder, for example – it wouldn't be an objection to his or her vocation, because the destiny of the vocation is the strength of Another who accomplishes it in me. The true problem is not the resolution "I won't murder anymore." The true resolution is "I entrust myself to You, I will rely on your strength," and in this way, I don't murder anymore (it's not that by doing this, I'm washing my hands!). The certainty of knowing how to arrive at not murdering, the certainty of being able to arrive at doing good, to avoid evil particularly in its worse moments, is due to the fact that You exist, that I entrust myself to You, implore You. For this reason, we can't be excused if we betray the vocation or if we suspend the energy that the vocation puts in all things. We cannot be excused because no weakness holds up in front of the strength of the One who called us: "You called me, You will carry me all the way to the end." If one says this with certainty, and asks for this every day, asks the Lord every day, "it will yield its fruit in due season."[22] What is its due season? It is that which is established by the One we belong to, like the apostles who asked Jesus: "Master, when will you end the world and give us the power?" "As to this day, no one knows, not even the Son of Man and not even the angels of God, but only the Father."[23] If this is true for the end of the world, it's true for the impulses of sanctity in me. Therefore I don't measure, I can't measure, you never measure; in the relationship with God, you never measure. This would be moralism – moralism measures everything. This is not a measurement, but a loving gaze, like the gaze that the apostles brought to Jesus. Most of them were married with children.

*Two brief lines from a witness fifteen days ago that several friends wrote to me as a summary of this period: "Instruct each other:*

*it's like an expressive formula of the event of friendship. What great riches of solicitousness, teaching, witness reside in our friendship, not for the discourses that are made, but for the life that exists and which you see."*

For the life that you live, for the facts more than for the words, because even the word is a fact: to say certain things, a struggle is required – in fact, not everyone says these things.

*What is the meaning of this sentence that you said: trust, which is the fulfillment of hope.*

What does it mean that trust is the fulfillment of hope? Having read a sentence, you must above all understand it.

*That it is the certainty that Another will bring about.*

Perfect. Trust is the certainty that Another will realize the ideal, man's just plan.

*Trust, which is the hope in its fulfilled expression, makes the "I" the principle of a new history in the world, the creator of a people.*

It makes the I the principle of a new history in the world, it allows it to act; only certainty allows someone to act; moreover, only definitive certainty makes someone act against everyone and against everything. Only definitive certainty gives the courage, the force, and the faithfulness to create, to generate. What a woman must undergo to generate applies to any form of generation. But it's not a human generating unless it is carried out as the creation of a people, unless it is a collaboration to create a new people, that is, a new humanity, but a real humanity.

One who has the vocation has such a human energy that it makes him or her capable of discovering the beauty of a fresco by Giotto, which others look at a hundred times more superficially or a hundred times more technically. One who looks at Giotto in this way edifies people to whom he explains that fresco; that is, he makes them different, places a little brick on a new construction. The culture that is now taught in school and on TV is completely lacking in this, it's no longer a people; they are all a herd of big sheep. But one who would go on television making the impression that Anna is capable of making when commenting on Giotto, would last five minutes; in those five minutes, people who would listen, would change, would feel that something is happening in them. If this would be continuous, television would create a new people.

But if, in a town, there is a house of Gruppo Adulto that lives its vocation (there can be houses in which people live like any other of the bourgeoisie; then, they don't have any impact, they don't have that introductory and intermediary reverberation of witnessing) in that town something new exists and grows, and you see it in one, in the other, in the other, not in everyone equally.

*Why do you say that to generate isn't a human generation if it does not generate a people?*
Above all, a creation isn't truly human if it doesn't create a people inasmuch as, generating even one single person, a principle of further generation is initiated. By its nature, a generation doesn't ever finish, it always expands, it's destined to always expand. And it is only the concept of family

that "concludes" the idea of generation; the generative idea is in the concept of family. The family is, in miniature, a people. But if a family is closed in on itself, it is no longer a generator, even if it has nine children; to be a generator, a family must be open to the possibility that it communicates itself to others, that it creates other families. It might not create other families; for example, two can be married without having children, but they live their humanity in such a way that they communicate to other families in the block of houses something that makes the others have thoughts, feelings, gestures that are more human: this is a dawn, a beginning of a new people.

The second reason is stated in the third volume of the School of Community,[24] where it answers the question of whether the value of the Church lies in the particular Church or in the total Church. I said: either it is in the total Church or else it is not in any Church. The particular Church does not have the capacity of catholicity, of totality; it doesn't have the capacity to express a meaning of everything, because, being a particular Church, it exalts its particular aspects, its circumstances. Only the universal Church, that is, the Church as a unity around the Pope, only that is truly a culture that challenges the culture of the world. Even in the world, a culture is that which claims to be communicable to all peoples, so much so that every revolution has, by instinct, the claim of universality. "Workers of the world, unite." Hitler dreamt of the world becoming Aryan: every revolution has a universal claim. The only universal claim that is fulfilled, fulfilled even among three who live in a little house, secluded, is the

Church. Therefore, a person who doesn't have a con-sciousness or a conception or a sense of that totality is not part of a people, and is not the source of a people, is not a facilitating factor for bringing one to the reality of a people: this is adequately given only by faith.

No humanity exists if there is not a heart that reaches out towards the farthest ends of the earth, if there is no meaning that is valid for all of the world in all of history, in all times. There wasn't even a people then, except for Attila's people, but we see where that led!

*In this year's journey, a new consciousness is coming about; in this way, I'm working in such a way that even the others comment on it to me.*
Great. When this happens, it is the beginning of the birth of a new people (maybe it will stop there, through the fault of others).

*But this evening, when you said these three points, it created a new rebellion in me.*
If it's a new rebellion, it could be the beginning of a new people!

*I don't even know how to explain it. The rebellion that sprang up inside of me posed a question: how do I adhere with my freedom to this rebellion that I feel?*
Rebellion towards what, towards the three points?

*Yes.*
Why a rebellion? First of all, why a rebellion?

*Rebellion, because these three points seemed new to me.*

It's not really a reason for rebellion – newness isn't a reason for rebelling. But you rightly call rebellion something that startles you, because you've never thought of those things – you understand? Now, the fact that you've never thought of those things before initially makes you feel strange, like a person who speaks another language. But if you think about it, is it true that we belong to Another or not? Is it true that the companionship that He puts us in reminds us of this or not? What does the companionship remind us of? Of this Other – you are the possession of this Other, you belong to this Other and this Other forgives you (forgives you, and if you make a mistake a hundred thousand times, He forgives you a hundred thousand times: this is precisely God, you must be God to do something like this!). Is it difficult?

*No, now I understand.*

But you understood even before, it's only that the shock of the diversity of new words blocked you, blocked you and gave you something like an impulse of refusal, or better, of strangeness. You felt left out by those words that I was saying. But if you go back to them, they are the things that we've been saying all year, they're the most reasonable things that you can say. Tell me a sentence more reasonable than this: man is a possession of God, belongs to God, to the Mystery; the Mystery creates a companionship to sustain man in his thinking of Him, otherwise man becomes scattered; and in this companionship he is forgiven; if he makes a million mistakes, not a hundred thousand but a million, he's forgiven a million times. There's nothing more rational than this, there's nothing more human than this. Last week, in a psalm, we read this: "Even if your father and mother would abandon you, I will never abandon you."[25] That is to say: there is no one more human than I.

*I was struck last week by your call for us to look Christ in the face, because it seems to me that there's nothing more beautiful to desire than this. But I ran the risk during this time of something akin to contemplating a holy card.*

This was a risk for me, too, in freshman year of high school, when I put the face of Christ by Carracci – who was not a very great painter – on the table, but it reminded me of Christ.

*But this came to mind: John and Andrew had a Presence before them and they went about their affairs with this Presence before them. Their faith was the certainty of a perceptible Presence.*
*So I want to understand better what it means for us to look Christ in the face.*

John and Andrew had faith, because they had certainty in a perceptible Presence. When they were there, in the first chapter of Saint John, seated at His house, toward evening, looking at Him speak, there was a certainty in a perceptible Presence of something exceptional, of the divine in a perceptible Presence. Then – I'm adding – they went home to sleep: Andrew to his wife, John to his mother. They went home, they ate at their home, they slept at their home, they got up, they went fishing together with the others in their group. What they had seen the afternoon before was dominating their minds – yes or no? Yes. Were they seeing Him? No.

But man experiences, has the experience of a presence, not only when he touches it, face to face; moreover, this way of wanting to experience a presence normally establishes something useless, it establishes a relationship that doesn't work – as is the case between all boys and girls – even when it works, it doesn't work. Instead, between the previous day and noon when they returned home with boats full of fish and they sat down there on the beach and were still relating the things that had happened the day before, the segment that relates the previous evening to the day after is called memory. Memory is the continuation of the experience of a present, the continuation of the experience of a person who is present, of a presence that no longer has the qualities and immediacy of when one grabs someone's nose and pulls, pulls, pulls, or else takes his hair and pulls his hair as children do with their mothers – that immediacy absolutely doesn't decide the depth and confidence of the relationship. They wouldn't have seen Him again for another three weeks; the dominant desire for those two was to go to see Him again, because it was clear that it was He, that He was He. They didn't know who He was, but it was He.

Memory is the awareness of a Presence. Concerning this Presence, you must distinguish when it began by what came after. When it began you saw His hair, and since there was wind and His hair got in His eyes, one instinctively pulls His hair to the side. But the day after, there was no more wind and they didn't have that face in front of them; nevertheless He was present. After a week, that Presence was Presence again, and after a month, Presence again; three years had gone by without seeing Him, all of their lives had been torn by the desire to see His hair again blown about in the wind: but that was He, an absolute certainty. The last – as all who want to be too concrete are abstract – the last thought that would have come to mind to those two (they wouldn't have seen Him again for six months) would have been the doubt that it had been an illusion. It never would have come into their minds that it was an illusion: for someone who had seen Him like this … impossible that this should come to mind.

Instead of Him with His hair in the wind, instead of watching Him speak with His mouth opening and shutting, He arrives through our presence, which is like fragile masks, fragile skin, the fragile masks of something powerful, which is He who lies within – not I or him or you, but something that nevertheless passes through me, passes through you, passes also through Him – and the things of today that no one tells you about. They aren't mine, they are His, He who Andrew and John were watching speak on that afternoon; He spoke and spoke, and in that way, conquering time and space, he spoke to you; and he will speak to you the day after tomorrow and in ten years from now.

And only if you commit some particular and serious error, before feeling forgiven, can you find refuge, as relief or attempted relief, in the idea that the encounter that you had was an illusion. Until you can compare what we tell you with everything others tell you, you can't ever say with seriousness that what we say is an illusion, because it conforms too well to your flesh and blood.

*I would like some help in understanding better this awareness of being a sinner, because two things happen to me: first, if I arrive at the end of the day, it's easier to see his mercy on me and it's more difficult to be aware of my sin; and second, one time you told us that forgiveness coincides with the companionship; so I know that sin exists, because the companionship exists, but this doesn't help increase the awareness of sin in me. And this is serious – I would like some help.*

There are two questions. The first: the evening, in the peace of the evening, it's easier to see mercy than to feel yourself a sinner. But if you have to feel mercy, it's because you made a mistake; you cannot feel yourself to be the object of mercy without implying that you have done something wrong. But this will have much more effect, my friend, the older you get; that is, the more mature you become in thinking about yourself. If in the evening when you feel mercy – "Of the mercy of the Lord the earth is full"[26] – you repeat this sentence with utmost attention ... what does it mean "Of the mercy of the Lord the earth is full?" That the Lord forgives everything that you do against Him, above all, forgetfulness. I, today – my God, what forgetfulness; I didn't offer what I could have offered ..." And then what? I wouldn't advise you to reason like that; if you go on with that type of reasoning, you have to say: "Oh yeah, I didn't treat my mother very well, and I was very superficial with my friends ..." and you make an enormous list for the whole evening. No. it's better to say: "Of your mercy, Lord the earth is full, thank you for your mercy on me." But you must say this keeping in mind that mercy is forgiveness for something that was done, even if that thing doesn't come to mind. Do you understand? Then, you're grateful, you're humble. It's not a specific and precise sorrow as if you had seriously offended your mother and she cried; this stays with you also in the evening and makes it difficult to think that God forgives you, it becomes difficult to even think about mercy. So, to think about mercy, you must really be sorrowful: but this type of sorrow isn't necessary, rather it is the awareness of being full of limits. Because your life could be one big praise of the Lord, your life could be enthusiastic about Christ, your life could be a reflection of the gaze that John and Andrew brought to Christ; your heart could be vibrating with that Presence which is the object of faith, the object of experience – but instead, no. Acknowledging this absence of yours, of course you feel humble, more humble; sorrow is hinted at as humility and it says: "Lord, I thank you for having mercy on me."

The second question. Forgiveness exists because the Lord forgives. And the Lord is so loving of man, is so loving towards us that, having to wait until the end of time to show Himself in all His evidence, being hidden now – as we said at the Ascension – from the root of things, He gave His Spirit as a support to us and as a help in our faithfulness to Him, help in our faithfulness to Him. In chapters 14, 15, and 16 of Saint John, doesn't He speak about the Spirit? "I will not leave you orphans, I will send my Spirit,"[27] but what is His Spirit? It is what these people around me let me see, not as anyone else would see: all your friends would see it in another way – all of them, even your father and mother – I, no. As soon as I am a little attentive, I say: these are people that the Lord places near me, part of me (baptism makes us part of His mysterious body, it makes us part of His person, a member of His body); therefore, being together with this companionship is precisely being immersed in the presence of Christ physically witnessed to, because what created that motion or that motive for which you're here is Another, this is not normal. It is Christ who moved your life until now, He called you in baptism, He made you encounter something that struck you, He put you together; it is Christ who expresses Himself inside this whole history. You don't condemn me because I make mistakes – I make mistakes just as you do – you don't condemn me, and the fact that I am embraced by your presence and made an object of attention for your merciful eyes and your hearts is precisely the sign of the fact that He watches me, that He embraces me, that He carries me, that He changes me, that He calls me back: all the verbs inherent to our companionship. In you, Christ is made perceptible, touchable, as the Pope said in his speech to the Roman youth:[28] He makes Himself touchable, visible, audible. But where was this already contained? In the first letter of Saint John.[29] Because you are part of Christ, so much so that we are part of each other; "you don't know that you are members of each other?"[30]

This is a realization of that universality that all the revolutionary theories dreamed of, but did not certainly realize; in the Church it is fulfilled: that we are all one. "All you who eat the same bread are one thing only, all you who were baptized have been made one with Christ; there is no longer Jew nor Greek nor slave nor free man nor man nor woman, but all of you are *eis,* one, one person only, who is called Christ Jesus."[31]

But, my friend, you must live it again; therefore the most correct thing that you said is "to take it more seriously." It's not only because I am comfortable with a person or I like him, but because that person "is"; without making any comparisons, this goes for comfort, for likes or dislikes, even if comfort and likes or dislikes remain.

May the grace of the Spirit let us understand that the ultimate meaning of all of this lies in the word sacrament: the companionship in its mysterious truth is a sacrament of which Baptism is the spring, the source, and the Eucharist is the ultimate event of verification of that mysterious truth.

*I would like to ask further why trust is certain.*

Trust is generated by our certainty that the object of our hope, happiness, will be given us – because God died for that. Certainty of hope coincides with the certainty of that abandonment that is called trust.

The Sardinian child is good all year, and nearing Christmas, writes a note to Baby Jesus: "Dear Baby Jesus, I was a good boy all year; so for Christmas, I'm asking you for Gullit's soccer ball and Laver's racket." Christmas comes and the two gifts aren't there. So he says: "I guess it must be for next Christmas." He is good all year – in his way, you understand – next December comes and he writes a letter to Jesus: "Dear Baby Jesus, last year, you didn't listen to me; this year, you have to listen to me, I was a good boy this year too. Therefore, can you bring me Gullit's soccer ball and Laver's racket?" Christmas comes, and he doesn't bring these presents at all. The Sardinian child (Sardinian!) stews inside for the whole year. Christmas comes; nine days before, Nativity scenes are put up; looking around, there's no one in sight, he grabs the baby out of the crib of the first Nativity scene he sees, he puts it in his pocket then he writes a letter: "Dear Blessed Mother, if you want your baby back, you have to let me have Gullit's soccer ball and Laver's racket."

Evidently, it's the same system, but in different fields.

In faith, certainty concerns the essence of the question. If I am at school, waiting for four o'clock in the afternoon in order to go home – back then, it was like that, morning and afternoon – to see my mother again, it was an absolute certainty. It's even more profoundly certain that God loved me, so much so that He became a man like me, 2000 years ago, staying with me every day, staying with men each day of history.[32] It's not necessary to know how it's possible for Him to exist, to be there; what's important is that you can't find a reason to say the opposite – the important thing is that He exists.

This is so true that, with this hypothesis, everything slowly changes and one arrives at a wisdom and a human affectivity that others dream about. For example: Albert Schweitzer – as you'll read in the book by Cesbron[33] – dedicated himself to others from the morning to the evening (a huge effort) and reached the evening sad. He had to vent his feelings at the piano to somewhat soothe the sadness, or in discussion with the nurse, where it didn't soothe the sadness but only heightened it. When Father Charles De Foucauld – who like him, lived among the natives, among the Africans, a little farther away, in the Touareg, in the south of Libya – passed by like a fleeting shadow, Schweitzer said to him: "But how can you be so happy? And how can those Africans love you so much, while here, they don't have affection for me, I who have dedicated all of my life for their well-being; nor do I feel affection for them? Meanwhile you who don't do anything for them, you stay with them and that's it, you eat with them, live with them, just like them (there is the book of his story entitled *Au coeur des masses*[34]) – why are you in such a different position?" The deep and just jealousy of the intelligent and great man that sees his dream realized in another present, a dream that cannot be fulfilled in him.

So, the certainty of hope is completely turned upside down in the abandonment of trust; therefore, trust is certain, trust carries with it, draws with it, a certainty that gladdens the heart even in the worst moments, which is the point of reference even amidst tears due to hardship (as we've read hundreds of times in the letters that arrive from all of the communities, fascinating witnesses of this exceptional Presence that acts among us).[35]

The certainty of trust is nothing but the corollary, the consequence, of the certainty of hope. What is hope? The certainty that it will happen, a certainty about the future. What does it rest on? On the certainty of a present. "I tell you: you will see the heavens open up and the Son of Man."[36] "I tell you this," so everything coheres and stands firm on a present experience: a present experience, almost the encounter with something unthinkable, unimaginable, not completely decipherable, because John and Andrew didn't understand well what that man they were watching speak in that little house in Galilee was saying, but it was clear that He was speaking the truth. So much so that upon returning home, they told others certain things that He had said: "We have found the Messiah."[37] But they didn't understand what the Messiah meant, they didn't even understand after he had died; for that reason, the first thing they asked Him after His resurrection, after the first extraordinary impact, was: "When will you make us leaders of your kingdom?"[38] They still had the same mentality as the others. And Christ didn't answer: "You don't even know what you're talking about!" but answered their question precisely: "Regarding these things, no one knows, not even the Son of Man, but only the Father who is in the heavens."[39] That day is a mystery – the day dreamed about by Camus[40] – that grace that invests everything, that sun, that daybreak, that day that comes not through our breathless labour, but as a great grace.

But – excuse me if I add this – how does one, a little man, him, me, endure something like this for years, years, and years, carrying along hundreds and hundreds of people? Whose strength is it? Ours? No, it's something else, it's a new world that inserts itself into the old world and proceeds like a stream of water that cuts through the earth and opens up the passageway like a brook or river does, until it reaches the sea. Then, it will be wonderful, great, to swim in it – no, better: we'll surf in it!

# Notes

## CHAPTER 1

1 Habakkuk 2: 4.

2 *See* Romans 1:17; Galatians 3:11; Hebrews 10:38.

3 "So to myself I cry: and of the vast/ Majestical abode,/ And of the family innumerable;/ Then of the mazy toil, the mazy motions/ Of all celestial, all terrestrial things,/ Circling in ceaseless rings,/ Ever returning whence they took their start:/ Of these can I divine/ No use, no fruit." "Night Song of a Nomadic Shepherd in Asia." In *The Poems of Leopardi*. Geoffrey L. Bickersteth, trans. and ed. Cambridge: Cambridge University Press 1923. 275.

4 "'Brother, will I bore you now, if I speak?'/ 'Speak: I can't sleep.' 'I hear gnawing, hardly ...' 'Maybe it's a woodworm ...'/ 'Brother, did you just hear a cry/ long, in the dark?' 'Maybe it's a dog ...'/ 'There are people outside the door ...' 'It must be the wind ...'/ 'I hear two soft, soft, soft voices ...'/ 'Maybe it's the rain that falls so sweetly.'/ 'Do you hear those taps?' 'It's the bells.'/ 'Are they announcing a death? are they hammering?'/ 'Maybe ...' 'I'm afraid ...' 'So am I.' 'I think it's thundering: / what will we do?' 'I don't know, brother: / Stay next to me: we're in peace: good.'/ 'I'll keep talking, if you're happy./ Remember, when through the lock/ the light

came in?' 'And now the light's out.'/ 'Even that time we were afraid: / yes, but not too much.' 'Now nothing comforts us,/ and we are alone in the dark night.'/ 'Remember? Now we aren't in peace/ so much, between us ...' 'Now we are better ...'/ 'Now there is no one who enjoys/ us ...' 'and no one who forgives us.'" G. Pascoli, "I due orfani." In *Poesie*. Milan: Garzanti 1974: 269–72.

5   Homily of 30 April 1983, published by the editors of *Insieme notizie*, bulletin of the Archdiocese of Bologna.

6   *See* Charles Péguy, *The Portico of the Mystery of the Second Virtue*. Dorothy Brown Aspinwall, trans. Metuchen: Scarecrow Press 1970. 12.

7   "Before the Break of Daylight," hymn of Thursday morning prayer. *Book of Hours*. Milan: Nuovo Mondo 1992. 132–3.

8   Mark 3:21.

9   Philippians 1:6.

10  Editor's note: He is referring to his own Lombard dialect.

11  Psalm 4:9.

12  *See* Luigi Giussani, *The Religious Sense*. John Zucchi, trans. Montreal and Kingston: McGill-Queen's University Press 1997. 7–9.

13  *See* John 21:15–17.

14  Giussani is referring to the speech of Mons. Dionigi Tettamanzi, then Secretary-General of the Italian Episcopal Conference, to the National Assembly of the Compagnia delle Opere, Milan, 12 February 1994. Compagnia delle Opere is a network of profit and non-profit companies inspired by Catholic social doctrine. It grew out of the experience of Communion and Liberation.

15  "The object of hope is a future good that is arduous but possible to attain." Thomas Aquinas, *Summa Theologiae*, II, II[ae], q. 17, a. 1.

16  *See* John 1:35ff.

17  Luke 7:36–50.

18  Luke 9:1–10.

19  Psalm 18:2.

20  Philippians 4:13.

21  *See* John 14:15–18.

22  Luke 21:19.

23  *See* Giussani, The Religious Sense. 59.

24  Giussani, *The Religious Sense*. 68–9.

25  *See* Charles Péguy, "The Portico of the Mystery of the Second Virtue." 123–6.

26  Romans 4:18.

27  *See* Giussani, *The Religious Sense*. 40–1.

28  (Ref.) Oh! doux pays de Chanaan, / qu'il est long le chemin vers toi! / Oh! doux pays de Chanaan, / doux pays de notre espoir. // Le temps me semble long et gris / au souvenir de ce doux pays, / Mais cette nuit nous partirons / vers le pays de la moisson. // Ref. // J'entends le son des tambourins / menant la dance jusqu'au matin, / en souvenir du doux agneau / dont le sang pur coula à flots. // Ref. // Nous passerons des nuits d'effroi / dans un desert glace des vents froid; / mais la Nuée est à l'entour / pour nous bruler d'un feu d'amour. // Ref. // Dans le matin d'un jour radieux / salut enfin, ô porte des cieux; / la pour toujours nous chanterons / le grand Hallel de la moisson. // Ref.

( (Ref.) O sweet land of Canaan, how long the road that leads to you! O sweet land of Canaan, sweet land of our hope. // Time seems long and gray / at the memory of that sweet land, / but we will leave tonight / for the land of the harvest. // Ref. // I hear the sound of tambourines / which lead the dance until morning, / in memory of the sweet lamb / whose pure blood gushed forth. // Ref. // We will pass nights of affliction / in an icy desert of freezing winds, / but the Cloud is present / to make us burn with a fire of love. // Ref. // In the morning of a radiant day, at last salvation, oh gate of the heavens; / there forever we shall sing/the great Alleluia of the harvest.)

29  Genesis 15:2.

30  M. Delafosse, *Les Noirs de l'Afrique*. Paris: Payot 1922. 153.

31 Mircea Eliade, *History of Religious Ideas*.Volumes 1–3. Willard R. Trask, trans. Chicago: University of Chicago Press 1978, 1982, and 1985.

32 Editor's note: Giussani is referring to Julien Ries, Professor Emeritus at the Catholic University of Louvain, a renowned historian of religion.

33 Genesis 14:18–20.

34 Plato, *Phaedo*. 85 c–d.

35 Psalm 73:9.

36 P.F. Lagerkvist, *Herod and Mariamne*. Naomi Walford, trans. New York: Vintage Books 1982.

37 *See* John 11:45–46.

38 *See* Matthew 18:3; Mark 10:15; Luke 18:17; John 3:3.

39 *See* Acts 1:6–7.

40 *See* Philippians 4:4.

41 John 15:11.

42 *See* Luke. 7:9.

43 "Our hearts are restless until they can find peace in you." St Augustine, *The Confessions* Book I:1,1. Rex Warner, trans. New York: New American Library 1963. 17.

44 *See* John 14:6.

45 *See* John 15:5.

46 See Luke 10:21.

47 Editor's note: Giussani is referring to the period in which young people who are considering a vocation to the consecrated life "test" this vocation, attending regular retreats and referring to a vocational company.

48 Philippians 1: 6

49 "Answer me, O God above in death's jaws: Can human will, summed, avail no fraction still of salvation?" H. Ibsen, "Brand" act V scene iii. F.E. Garrett, trans. London: J.M. Dent & Sons 1924.

50 Editor's note: This refers to the first year of the novitiate of Memores
   Domini.

51 *Didache*, IV, 2.

52 *See* John 14:9.

53 "To his Lady." In *The Poems of Leopardi*. Geoffrey L. Bickersteth,
   trans. and ed. Cambridge: Cambridge University Press 1923. 237.

54 Thomas Mann, *Joseph in Egypt*. H.T. Lowe-Porter, trans. New
   York: Knopf 1938. 37.

55 "Between offering and fulfillment there is always a kind of contrast,
   an error, an oversight." A. von Speyr, *Mistica oggettiva*. Milano: Jaca
   Book 1975. 249.

56 *See* Giussani, "The Journeying." In Giussani, *He Is if He Changes*
   (supplement to 30 *Days* 7/8 1994). 24.

57 J. Ratzinger, *Che cosa crede la Chiesa*, in *Il Sabato* (5) 30 January
   1993.

58 *See* Philippians 4: 13.

CHAPTER 2

1 *See* Luke 12:16–21.

2 Philippians 1:6.

3 Editor's note: gladness is the approximate translation of *letizia* (*liesse*
   in French), which conveys joy, gladness, and delight.

4 François Mauriac, *Life of Jesus*. Julie Kernan, trans. New York:
   Longmans, Green and Co. 1937. 63–4.

5 *See* 1 Corinthians 7:29–31.

6 *The Little Flowers of St. Francis*. Chapter 8.

7 Luigi Giussani, *The Religious Sense*. John Zucchi, trans. Montreal
   and Kingston: McGill-Queen's University Press 1997. 114.

8 Giussani, "1981: La fine di un mondo." In *Un avvenimento cioè una
   storia*. Rome: EDIT Il Sabato 1993.143–4.

9 Editor's note: The *Pirellone* is the nickname the Milanese give to the Pirelli office tower, the tallest building in Milan.

10 *See* Giussani, *The Religious Sense*. 124.

11 N. Salvaneschi, *Sorella Chiara*. Milan: Dall'Oglio 1954. 5.


## CHAPTER 3

1 Cfr. Matthew 7:11; Luke 11:13.

2 "If you believe in god and no god exists,/ then your belief is an even greater wonder./ Then it is really something inconceivably great./ Why should a being lie down there in the darkness crying to someone who does not exist?/ Why should that be?/ There is no one who hears when someone cries in the darkness. But why does that cry exist?" Pär Lagerkvist. In *Eveningland aftonland*. W.H. Auden and Leif Sjöberg, trans. Detroit: Wayne State University Press 1975. 127.

3 John 14:6.

4 Milan Kundera, *The Unbearable Lightness of Being*. London: Faber and Faber 1987. Editor's note: Giussani is referring to Adelphi, the Italian publisher of the work.

5 1 Corinthians 7:29–35.

6 Psalm 48.

7 He is referring to Angelo Scola, *Laity: ie, Christians. An Interview with Luigi Giussani*. Milan: Nuovo Mondo 1988. 7–8.

8 Luigi Giussani, "L'idea di movimento." In *Un avvenimento di vita cioè una storia*. 346.

9 Philippians 4:13.

10 Giussani, "L'io e la grande occasione." In *Dalla fede il metodo*. Milan: Nuovo Mondo 1994. 14.

11 1 John 1:8–9.

12 Editor's note: Giussani is referring to a weekly meeting of each Memores Domini home.

13 Psalm 119:45-8.

14 Psalm 128.

15 *See* Mark 13:32.

16 The songs mentioned are contained in the *Songbook* of Communion and Liberation.

17 "And weep'st thou not, what art thou wont to weep at?" *Inferno*. canto XXXIII, 42. Longfellow translation.

18 *See* 2 Peter 3:9.

19 Como busca el tierno infante / afligido y pesaroso, / el descanso y el reposo / en el seno maternal, / asi yo, desde que brilla / la luz blanca de la aurora / vengo a buscar, oh Señora, / tu protection celestial. (As the tender child who is worried and agitated seeks rest and peace at its mother's breast, so do I, from the first white light of dawn, come to seek, O Blessed Mother, your heavenly protection).

20 Beethoven, Concerto for Violin and Orchestra. op. 61.

21 *See*, in this chapter, the fourth point: "Conscious of time."

22 Psalm 1:3.

23 Mark 13:32.

24 Giussani, *Why the Church?* Vivianne Hewitt, trans. Montreal and Kingston: McGill-Queen's University Press 2001.

25 *See* Isaiah 49:14; Psalm 27:10.

26 *See* Psalm 32:5.

27 John 14:18.

28 John Paul II, speech to Roman youth, 24 March 1994. Supplement to 30 *Giorni*, (4), April 1994.

29 *See* 1 John 1:1.

30 Ephesians 4:25; Romans 12:5.

31 Galatians 3:27-8.

32 See Matthew 28:20.

33 Gilbert Cesbron, *Il est minuit Docteur Schweitzer*. Paris: Laffont 1952.

34 René Voillaume, *Au coeur des masses. La vie religieuse des petits frères du Père de Foucauld*. Paris: Editions du Cerf 1950. Translated as *Seeds of the Desert*. Notre Dame: Fides Dome 1964.

35 Editor's note: Giussani is referring to letters published in the magazine *Traces*, the official review of Communion and Liberation.

36 John 1:51.

37 John 1:41.

38 Acts 1:6.

39 Acts 1:7.

40 "Ce n'est pas avec des scrupules qu'un homme deviendra grand. La grandeur vient au gré de Dieu, comme un beau jour." (It is not with scruples that a man will become great. Greatness comes about, God willing, like a beautiful day.) Albert Camus, *Carnets III mars 1951-décembre 1959*. Paris: Gallimard 1989. 37.